# SUPERSCROOGE
## 3000 SNEAKY WAYS
## TO SAVE MONEY

**Malcolm Stacey is a Yorkshireman . . .
Need we say more?**

# SUPER SCROOGE

## 3000 SNEAKY WAYS TO SAVE MONEY

# MALCOLM STACEY

*Illustrations by Pat Drennan*

QUILLER PRESS

*To my parents, Douglas and Hilda,*
*who taught me all I know.*

First published by Quiller Press Ltd
46 Lillie Road
London SW6 1TN

Reprinted 1991

ISBN: 1 870948 49 1

Produced by Hugh Tempest-Radford Book Producers
Printed in Great Britain by The Bath Press

# Contents

# Acknowledgements

Jo Perkins, Alice Moulding, Doug Waring, Richard Stacey, Cathy Fletcher, Daniel Jodey-Michaels, Ian Dick, Leslie Watts, Barney Wordsworth, John Howard, Debbie Higgins, Keith Jones, Shirley Cummings, David Berry, Hazel Castell, Henry Russell, Mike Stewart, Rod McCrae, Cyril Mitchell, James Watt, Nance Parry and John Dimmock.

(Actually, few on this list were any use whatsoever. But it's hoped they're keen enough to see their names in print to go out and buy at least two copies. I'm certainly not giving any away.)

# Introduction

Hear all, see all, say nowt,
Eat all, sup all, pay nowt,
And if ever tha does owt for nowt,
Alus do it for thisen.
—*Old Yorkshire proverb*

IF you're that wise kind of person who sees perfect sense in the above philosophy, and is sufficiently interested in the theme of this book to take it from the shelf, you'll already be wondering if you can avoid buying it. By merely reading this introduction, and putting it back, perhaps.

One sympathizes, of course, but you'll be passing up a lifetime's opportunity — to live like royalty without earning more than you do now.

You see, this practical guide isn't about scrimping and saving in a way which will make your life a misery. You won't begin an existence like the opening chapter of *A Christmas Carol*. Neither is it a compendium of petty ideas which might just save you a few pennies, if you work hard enough.

Some volumes on thrift tell you to crochet a dishcloth from old bits of string. Or make an overcoat from a blanket. Or use newspaper in the toilet. This one won't.

What it will do is help you to make your income go much further, so that you can live in some style, while others, who earn more, continue to struggle on.

They'll think you are a secret pools winner.

It's not about saving, but obtaining everything you want in life, by paying less. You'll learn how to play the system and sponge on relatives and friends.

But as these activities can ostracize you from society, I'll also tell you how to avoid being found out. Follow the thousands of tips in these pages, and not only will you spend much less on a fuller life, but you'll appear very generous to boot.

I've never earned more than an average wage in my life, but I own three houses, two vintage cars, and hundreds of antiques. I'm not dishonest. I pay my taxes. Nobody thinks I'm stingy. But I get everything either cheap or free. These secrets are now yours.

This is a practical manual. But if there is a general theory behind the process of becoming affluent, it works like this. Flatmates Alex and Jo are paid the same. Alex pays £20 for a toaster, Jo gets it for £10. Jo is now £10 better off than Alex, but that money isn't taxed, so she's really £13.33p better off. Alex then shells out £25 for a hairdryer. Of course, Jo won't need a hairdryer because she can now borrow Alex's.

Alex incurs bank charges and interest because her current account keeps sliding into the red. Jo earns interest on her money.

Of course Jo prospers, while poor Alex has to cut back to avoid getting into debt.

You will see that to get on in the world you need to: (a) pay less to make money; (b) know how to make the most of that saving; and (c) take advantage of others.

In these pages, you'll learn how to apply all these principles to every area of living, including food, clothing, transport, work, enter-tainment, do-it-yourself and bringing up children. You'll become a fully fledged 'frugalist'. That's my word for someone who lives well at the expense of the system or other individuals. (It's important to coin an alternative expression to 'cheapskate', as this implies someone who suffers in the cause of personal economy.) Your life of luxury is about to begin.

Though some of my recommendations are straightforward, other stratagems are more devious, and may even appear fanciful. They all work, nonetheless.

It must be said that some of the ploys are underhand, but are never, ever, dishonest. Acting illegally would kill all the fun stone dead. You may also decide to practise some of the more outrageous ideas only on those who deserve it.

I've included plenty of simple ideas for economizing on almost everything, though more obvious money-savers you may have already heard about have been excluded.

Many of the techniques I describe can be adapted to all sorts of different situations.

The book includes a few time-saving suggestions. After all, time is money. And there's a section on easy ways of making extra cash, too.

But before we get to the nitty gritty, here's a list of ten useful maxims to set you on the right road to almost instant prosperity:

 Never shop for fun.

Buy second-hand.

It's better to receive than give.

A pound in time saves nine.

Never give your friends or relatives an even break.

Not a lender, but a borrower be.

Marry for love not money – but remember it's easier to love someone who's rolling in it.

A friend in need is a nuisance.

Where there's a will, make sure you're mentioned in it.

Christmas should be spent at home – someone else's.

And now you're getting the idea, let battle commence.

# Leisure

## . . . or How to Have a Good Time at Somebody Else's Expense

Economy is the art of making the most of life. The love of economy is the root of all virtue.

—*Bernard Shaw*

MOST of the population save money by staying in every evening watching TV. Yet only by getting out and about in style can you make work and social contacts vital to wealth and popularity. And you can easily have a rattling night out for a lot less than you think. There are stingy *bon viveurs* the world over who make sure others pay. They still manage to look and act like big spenders. Here's how.

### Ten Ways of Avoiding Paying for Your Round

 Stride purposely to the pub in front of the group. This means you will have to hold the door open while someone else moves to the bar first.

Try to be last in the party to buy drinks. The cost of a round reduces progressively as drivers switch to half pints, shandy and fruit juice.

With five people in the party, absent-mindedly mention that risks of heart attacks are cut down by having one glass of water for every four alcoholic drinks. Once again, make sure you are the last to pay the round.

The pocket-tapping ploy. Take the order while frantically feeling around your person for your purse or wallet. Look thoroughly miserable, as though it has been stolen. Sympathy dictates that someone else will pay.

As your turn approaches, say, 'There seem to be a few police cars about tonight.'

Seek out any other acquaintances in the pub. Go over to chat just before you are due to buy for those you came in with. Rejoin the original group when the danger is past.

Many pubs have a mini-phone in every bar nowadays. While pretending to visit the toilet, ring the nearest phone from another room. Ask if there is anyone with your name in the pub. The answerer will call your name out while you hang up and go round to answer the 'call'. Stay on the dead phone till your time to buy is well past.

Note the cheapest beer on sale. Just before your round, say you read recently that this brand won lots of awards for quality 'somewhere in Germany'.

Just before you can no longer put off your 'shout', suggest a change of pub. By the time you arrive, the previous buying order will be forgotten.

 Ask for an expensive tipple every time, until your turn comes round. Then order a cheap one. Others, not wanting to appear greedy, will follow your example.

Remember that, when buying your round, you can always put extra tonic or lager in your own glass to make a saving. Make up for it when others are paying.

Of course, if these tactics are followed slavishly in every pub you may damage your reputation. Dispel ugly rumours by buying a bottle of champagne once in a blue moon when it's your round. The popping cork will make a lasting impression of your perceived generosity.

Choose your pub carefully, though. Some only sell expensive brands of bubbly. And don't fret. Only one bottle every three years will do the trick.

There's also a play-on-words technique for getting a free drink. For example, you tell a companion at the bar you have just seen someone who looks exactly like yourself outside the Town Hall.

He says, 'Really, you must have a double.' You reply, 'Thanks, make it a scotch, please.'

I'm afraid this trick has yet to work for me.

## The Silver Screen

First ask yourself if you need to see this film *now*. It will be in video rental shops soon. Then the family, in-laws, lodgers, friends and neighbours could all see it for a third of the cost of one cinema ticket.

I have a deal with a neighbour who hands all his rented films to me for part of the evening. I reciprocate. In any case, the same film will soon be on TV for nothing.

If you prefer the big screen, you can still cut costs. Always go on a Monday when most cinemas reduce prices. Never buy tickets for the dearer seats. All you're paying extra for is a smaller screen (it's further away) and greater opportunities to see people moving about between you and the action.

It's cheaper to take your own nuts, crisps, orange squash and popcorn.

## How to Go to the Cinema for Nothing

Write to the manager saying you may never return after twenty years' loyal custom. This is because the sound track was too loud last time you came. Or there were too many adverts to sit through. In the interests of honesty, choose only a genuine reason. You'll get an apology and two complimentary tickets by return post.

Or ask the local free sheet newspaper if you can send in occasional film reports. Then correctly introduce yourself to your cinema manager as a film critic. He'll gladly let you in gratis.

Writing a film criticism calls for no previous experience, by the way. Simply tell a bit of the story. Then say it was magical, thrilling, side-splitting, a triumph for its stars and so on. Whether or not the paper prints your no-doubt amateur efforts is, of course, irrelevant.

There's also nothing to stop you starting your own arts magazine. Invent a title like 'Big Screen Gazette'. Write articles on cheap paper, run copies off and circulate them to your friends. Then you can approach the cinema manager as critic for 'Big Screen Gazette'. You never know, your magazine might take off.

The above methods of getting free cinema seats can be applied to live theatre. There are also other dodges you can use to save money on stage performances. As Government subsidies reduce, ticket prices can easily cost a day's wages, so the following tips are worth a go.

## How to Save Money at the Theatre

Book cheap seats high up in the 'gods', and come early. Confide to the manager that you have vertigo. You might fall, perhaps killing a few patrons below. You'll be relocated in better seats. Though sadly the royal box will be denied you.

When ordering cheap seats, make sure from the theatre plan they are behind a pillar. Arrive just before curtain-up. Start to make a noisy fuss because you cannot see. More than likely you will be urgently 'calmed down' by putting your whole party in good seats in a higher price band.

You should also tell your friends that you like to encourage what's known as the 'town and gown' relationship with your nearest university. This really means going to varsity shows and concerts, with very cheap tickets aimed at students.

Cultivate a taste for amateur productions. Tickets are cheaper and plays much funnier than professional performances. You could die laughing when the hero falls into the orchestra pit, followed by the scenery.

It also enhances your reputation as a man or woman about town to be seen at amateur first nights. The town's dignitaries will be there.

## How to Get the Best Theatre Seats Free

Write to a minor member of the cast of the opposite sex saying you have followed their career with admiration. You are delighted he or she is performing at last in your own town. But you're mortified that you can't get tickets on the only date available to you.

This is because you quail at spending the money. But he or she, with show business vanity, will assume your failure is because the house is full. Every performer gets free tickets. No doubt some of these will be sent on to you.

This next tip is elaborate and time-consuming, but satisfying

because you're being a Good Samaritan at the same time. Suggest to a home for the elderly that you would like to take their oldest resident to the theatre. Then inform the theatre's press officer of your plan to arrange Grannie Smith's first theatre outing for forty years.

Inquire if she can go back-stage afterwards to meet the cast. She would love to see her picture in the paper with these stars.

I guarantee that not only will the theatre come up with free seats for both of you on the first night, they'll also arrange transport. Perhaps even a Rolls-Royce. And you need nurse no troubled conscience. You're simply giving an elderly person a rare treat.

Another way to see theatre productions (and pop and classical concerts) for nothing is to join the St John's Ambulance Brigade.

## Eating Out with Friends

Going out for a meal is becoming even more popular. To foster your 'good living' image you should take friends, colleagues or contacts to a good restaurant at least once a week. But this sort of evening holds dangers for the dedicated frugalist. Without care, it will cost dear.

As a careful spender, you already know that restaurateurs shore up the final bill by overcharging for starters, sweets and liqueurs. Your fellow diners may not be aware of this dirty trick. It may reveal your parsimonious tendency if you reveal it. So while you discreetly decline the frills, the others may well order with ignorant abandon.

In these circumstances, sharing the total bill into equal parts at the end of the meal is not in your interests. So, before you eat, suggest that separate bills are provided, as you need your own receipt 'for tax reasons'.

Then decline a starter by saying you had a big lunch. Reject a sweet by pleading a diet. Tearfully turn down a liqueur because you are driving.

You can deal with any hunger pangs by scoffing all the bread and attacking extras like garlic bread, poppadoms and side dishes of vegetables and salads.

## Sharing the Final Bill

If you learn at an early stage you won't be able to avoid an equal share of the bill, you might as well eat everything you can. When the waiter looms with the final reckoning, offer to pay the lot by charge card. Then take the other diners' contributions in cash. Flushed with drink and bonhomie by this time, they will rarely ask for change.

To stay on the right side of honesty you announce, 'Well, that's a little over what the bill came to, so I'll see the waiter is all right.' Then you go over to the waiter and secretly ask, 'Are you all right?'

## *Other Tips on Cutting Restaurant Bills*

Italian and Chinese restaurants are usually cheaper than French ones.

Shun costly meat dishes by becoming a vegetarian (at least for the evening).

Suggest that 'we all do something trendy for a change'. Then lead everyone into a transport cafe.

## *Getting Another Diner to Pay for You*

When a waiter brings a bill, he'll hand it to the dominant male. Try to look small and oppressed at this point. Stare miserably at your boots. Blow your nose to make him think you are ill. Or search under the table for a supposedly lost coin.

You never know. The luckless person who ends up with the bill might make a magnanimous gesture and pay for everyone. Perhaps not very likely, but worth a try.

Women should never offer to pay for themselves when escorted in a restaurant by a man. Show your independence in hundreds of *other* ways. Conversely, men should gallantly bow to sex equality by engineering that the lady should pay her whack, and preferably his, too.

## *Dinner for Two?*

If you're trapped into paying for everything after a dinner for two in a swanky restaurant, here's how to keep down the cost:

 Assertively order the house wine, before your partner has the chance to discover the wine list.

Discourage expensive gluttony by saying, 'You look very trim tonight. You must have an iron will to keep a figure like that.'

If your guest looks like ordering lobster, wonder why it takes a minute for the poor creature to die in boiling water to get that lovely pink colour.

If caviar is on the menu, discuss the scandal of oceanic pollution near Russia. If oysters are dallied over, mention the latest shellfish scare.

Don't dominate the conversation. The more your guests talk the less they eat.

Recommend one of the cheapest offerings on the menu for its 'remarkable' lack of calories.

When you come across a dish with a foreign name that's over your limit, confess you don't speak the language but feel it might be something to do with horses.

Even at the risk of bad manners, put in your order for the cheapest dishes first. Your guest will find it difficult to go too far up the price table after your lead.

If you start by discussing the main courses, your guest will often forgo the starter when offered.

 Coffee and liqueurs can often be taken more comfortably (and cheaply) at home. Your guest's house, of course.

## *A Night on the Town*

Nightclubs are both expensive to get in, and costly to stay in. Because of hiked bar prices, a few slightly underhand, cost-reducing ploys are justified.

Fill a screw-top tonic bottle with gin. Take it into the club. Buy another bottle of tonic from the bar, which, of course, comes with a glass and ice. Mix your own G and Ts for the rest of the evening.

Just when your friends expect you to buy a round, rise from your seat to dance.

Drink two glasses of water before you arrive, so you won't get too thirsty bopping in a smoky atmosphere.

If the club advertises a Hallowe'en special or an Hawaiian evening you should negotiate with the management. Ask if they will let you in free if you help along the promotion by dressing up. A horror mask or a grass skirt should do it. Once inside, change back in the toilets to stop looking silly all night.

You should also avoid weekends when admission is higher. And take advantage of ladies' nights when women are allowed in free.

## *Nights Out for Nothing*

These fall into the category of 'home entertainment'. The trick is to make sure it is not *your* home. Invited guests not only deplete your booze, biscuits and coffee, they use up electricity, gas, carpet pile, washing-up liquid and soap. Overnight stayers whose sheets and towels need laundering are a real menace.

Getting yourself invited to a home-cooked meal is a good start. All that free sherry, food, wine and brandy. And no washing up! You can evade any expectation of a return engagement *chez nous* by lamenting, 'If only I could prepare lovely meals like this. Sadly, my cooking would make a goat sick.'

Suggest that a friend plays host to a card game. They'll provide drinks and nibbles, of course. Not only will there be no cost, you'll save on central heating and lighting at your house.

But only play a game, like poker, for money if you've been practising and have read definitive books on the subject. It goes without saying your opponents must be complete novices.

Big events on TV are ideal excuses to benefit from someone else's home comforts. Suggest that you come over to watch a general election programme, the European Song Contest, a royal wedding, the London Marathon or the Cup Final. It will, you simper, enhance the occasion to share it with such dear friends. Set pieces like the ITV Telethon or the BBC's Children in Need event should keep you fed, watered and warmed, on a comfortable sofa, for some time.

Persuade an acquaintance in the country to revive the Victorian custom of inviting friends (like you) to a weekend at home. Remind her that it was fashionable to call for visitors at the station in a pony and trap. But in this case a comfortable car will do.

## Parties

Going to a house party is one of the best ways of eating and drinking there is. It doesn't cost a penny. And the free food, especially around Christmas, New Year, Hallowe'en and bonfire night is more imaginative than any restaurant.

Sadly, custom and practice require us to take a bottle to parties. Here's how to avoid leaving it there.

 Brandishing a whisky bottle, walk up the hall, through the kitchen and out again through the back door. Stroll out the back gate or up the side passage and replace the bottle in your car.

Walk into the party with a bottle of champagne. Announce, 'This is too good to drink now. I'll hide it till later.' Secrete it under your overcoat in the bedroom. Walk out with both coat and bottle when you go home.

Approach the kitchen waving a bottle of wine in each hand. Greet the host. Then shriek, 'Goodness, I've left the lights on.' Rush back into the night. Quietly return, without the bottles.

 Steam the label from an expensive French wine and plaster it on a cheap Bulgarian. Or, better still, one of your home-made wines. (This is legal if you don't sell it on.) You can impress your hosts by flourishing this 'rare vintage' under their noses.

By the way, bringing Tizer in a whisky bottle isn't worth the considerable risk of being found out. Sadly, one knows this from experience.

## Golden Rules of Profitable Party-going

Don't arrive on a full stomach. How can you do justice to all that free food? The hosts will only be offended if any uncleared plates are left in the morning.

Take your own bottle-opener. It saves serious drinking time.

If you smoke, always offer a pack with only one cigarette in it. Your friends will shun taking your last and will instead offer you one of theirs. Keep a full pack in your other pocket for private consumption.

Never arrange to meet friends in a pub before going on to a party. Not only will this mar a *free* night out (unless you mastered the rules given earlier) but it's not very sophisticated to need Dutch courage to socialize.

Baby-sitters who raid your food and electricity, and, worse, want paying, are rarely necessary. Take babies and small children with you. Park them in spare bedrooms. Check from time to time that no one has dumped overcoats on top of them.

Take advantage of the small talk to discover who's holding a party next week. Mention that you might be available.

### NEVER, EVER, GIVE A PARTY YOURSELF

Sometimes a hostess will forget to invite you. But remember it's morally justified to crash a party if: (a) the official turnout is disappointing; (b) the invited guests are not as lively as you are going to be; or (c) the hostess was once rude to you.

## How to Crash a Party

Announce that you are a friend of John or Sarah. Someone with these popular names is bound to be present.

Armed with a clipboard, pretend to investigate a complaint about noise. Then grudgingly allow yourself to be persuaded to stay.

Assume the guise of a kissogram girl. Use your old school uniform. Accost the host in the usual manner. Then stay on afterwards.

Come late when the drink is in full flow. By now no one knows or cares who you are.

If about to be thrown out, make a fuss of the cat.

When crashing a fancy-dress party disguise yourself in a gorilla mask and grunt mysteriously when anyone talks to you. Bring a straw to drink with.

## How to Save Money on Fancy Dress

Costume balls and parties are expensive if you hire from a shop. Instead borrow the working gear of a teacher, nurse or bus conductor you know. If they refuse, you'll be congratulated on your imagination for trying one of the following easy-to-make, low-cost get-ups:

*Vicar*: dark suit, black shirt and cardboard dog-collar.

*Schoolgirl*: old school uniform.

*One-armed bandit*: one arm tucked inside a jacket with a string of three lemons round the neck.

*Punk rocker*: lots of safety pins and a bin-liner.

*Burglar*: striped jumper, sack of old tins and cardboard cut-out mask.

*Dice*: get a large cardboard box, paint it with leftover white gloss. Cut out black dots to stick on the sides. Loop the box over your shoulders with ribbon.

*Injured stuntman*: black trousers and shirt with arm in sling. A pinned placard should read 'and all because the lady loves Milk Tray'.

## Family Outings

Taking your nearest and dearest on an outing is a serious matter. It could cost you a bundle. But it need not. Instead of saving up for the racecourse, a bowling alley, the cinema or theatre, consider these low-cost alternatives:

A *museum or art gallery*. Only patronize those run by a local authority. Commercial exhibitions, including some waxworks and horror shows may be better publicized, but they're expensive. And sometimes short on exhibits to boot. While, contrary to public belief, all but a few of the top London museums and galleries – the envy of the world – are still gratis.

Any admission charge at a museum can be side-stepped, together with the whole family, by making an appointment with the curator to inspect an antique. Any old piece of junk will do. When she's done the business, ask, 'Would you mind if we have a look round while we're here?'

Or visit a *cathedral* or *ancient church*. This is free, except with rare exceptions like the best bits of Westminster Abbey. Some old places of worship are heaving with history. (It's not unusual to find the body of a king of England lying about.) Some churches even provide their own inexpensive catering.

Get a National Trust season ticket to see a lot of *castles, stately homes* and wonderful *gardens* in bulk. Buy a comprehensive book on historic monuments and always take it with you. This saves getting stung for an expensive guide book on each visit.

For some odd reason many councils are reviving a Victorian fashion for large glasshouses full of tropical plants and butterflies. These fascinating attractions are usually free, and warmly cheering on a winter's day.

You'll need a bank loan to take your family to the zoo nowadays, but you can glimpse many animals, especially lofty ones like giraffes, by strolling round the outside walls. London Zoo, in Regent's Park, is a good example.

## The Importance of Earnest Self-catering

Take your own food on a day out. The world is full of mobile vans and pseudo-genteel tea-rooms, supplying hapless tourists with health-threatening fry-ups they would probably never serve at home. Prices are inflated and so are the queues.

All this can be avoided by acquiring the habit of making sandwiches and filling thermos flasks. New picnic baskets are expensive. Once very fashionable, they turn up very cheaply in today's auctions.

In any event, you can always make a picnic kit from an old suitcase. Simply stitch elastic strips on the inside walls and base. Secure six plastic mugs, and six tea plates, with knives, forks and spoons inside. Plastic margarine and ice-cream tubs will hold the sandwiches and cake. These can be held in the same way.

I wouldn't want anyone to see me eating from a tatty suitcase, so keep it hidden in the boot. Carry a bright tablecloth to spread on the grass.

## By the Sea

Don't take the family to the coast unless sun is forecast. The beach is free, but your choices if it's wet are far from it. Amusement arcades and souvenir shops should be shunned. Childhood treats like the dodgems and big wheels are best left to pools winners.

If the day is threatening, it's best to take your tribe to one of those few remaining resorts which still demur at commercial enterprise.

Leave the car in a residential street, not a car park, and walk to the prom. Your own folding chairs will foil eagle-eyed deck-chair attendants.

Take your children to pat and stroke the donkeys. But hint they might get bitten if they ride on them. Watch Punch and Judy performances from a distance, and stroll away just before the show's end.

## A Free Day by the Sea

A foolproof way to get yourself, family and even a few friends to the coast for nothing is to organize a coach trip for people at work. All it takes is a bit of shopping around in the yellow pages. Find the cheapest coach and driver. A scruffy-looking vehicle will add to the fun. But ask for documentary evidence that the insurance is in order.

Take a list of names at work. Calculate the price of each fare. Add on a bit to pay for your family's tickets. Then a little extra for your trouble.

Collect the money well in advance in case people back out. All you have to do now is turn up at the appointed time with your own party, establish your role as organiser by sitting in the front seats, and off you go.

You'll later be asked to organize similarly lucrative outings to race meetings, greyhound tracks, discotheques and historical monuments. And you'll never look back.

## A Cheap Day in the Country

A day's rambling, especially if you take your own peanut butter sandwiches will cost . . . peanuts. Merely take a bus to a nearby beauty spot. Call in at a local newsagent for a paltry-priced map showing a few easy walks. And spend the rest of the day without airing your purse.

Horse shows and regattas occur often, and admission is as low at agricultural shows as entertainment values are high. There are lots of animals for children to see, and loads of brass bands and flowers for adult appreciation. And, unless you plan to breed Jerseys, there's hardly anything to buy.

# Work

*Frugality is a handsome income.*
*—Erasmus*

GOING to work is expensive. You have to pay bus and train fares, dress respectably, pay taxes, give to retirement collections, and perhaps stump up for a childminder.

Look on the bright side, though. While you're working you're not shopping. Eating is cheaper, if the canteen is subsidized. And your own home won't use up gas and electricity while you're away. You may get free calendars and diaries.

And there are myriad ways you can save money at work, without stealing telephone calls, paper cups and envelopes.

## Getting to Work

Expert frugalists know the social and economic advantages of getting a car with the job. Hold out for one at all costs. It saves so much expense. It looks so successful.

Failing this, you should jog to work. Not only does this cut out bus fares, but it shakes the wrinkles out of your suit. Alternatively, walking to work shares the same advantage of not having to exercise during valuable hours after work.

Or organize a colleague living nearby to pick you up and take you back. Always be ready on time, otherwise the arrangement won't last.

You could cycle to work. Don't buy a new machine. It'll be pinched. Luckily, second-hand ones are everywhere. (I hope that's nothing to do with the thefts.) Mine came from a home clearance warehouse for the price of a tyre on a new bike.

Try not to be seen in the saddle though. If you want promotion, park a few streets away.

Take advantage of an annual season ticket for buses and trains. Refunds are easy if you move or lose your job. But keep a photocopy, for a replacement if you lose it.

If something of value is to be left in the office or workshop overnight, offer to take it home where you can keep an eye on it.

Suggest that, for added security, a taxi is laid on . . . as it will be if you simply collapse over your desk towards home time. There's no need to lie about being ill. The assumption will be made.

## Dressing for Work

You'll earn more respect all round if you wear a smart suit. This instant prestige gives you a more powerful appearance, allowing you to delegate more, and work less. Clothes maketh the manager.

Grey is best for business suits on both men and women. It suggests self-confidence and dependability. People who keep their shoes polished and nails clipped get promoted more than others, too.

Sporting a bag with 'Harrods' or 'Gucci' written on it also helps.

## Eating at Work

Make full use of the subsidized works canteen. Breakfast there. Have lunch there. If possible have a cheap meal before you go home.

You may need excuses for those tiresome colleagues who say, 'Let's go out to eat for a change today.' Some suggested replies:

> 'I can't leave the building. I'm expecting a call from my doctor.'

> 'I have to watch my diet.' Then stare at your colleague's waistline, adding, 'Like quite a few of us around here.'

> 'I'd love to go out, but you'll have to pay. I've forgotten my credit card.' Well, you never know your luck.

The beauty of company canteens is that no one minds if you ladle on big portions. By taking a lot of one vegetable, instead of smaller amounts of three, you save money at the till. Have a double helping of soup and you won't need the pud. Or vice versa.

Eat with others. The bigger the lunch party, the more likely it is that somebody will be too full to eat his afters. Save face by proclaiming, 'Food should never be wasted.' Then tuck in.

Try not to be the first to finish your meal. The onus is on an early finisher to offer to buy a round of coffee.

In all probability, your firm won't actually write down any rules about who should use the canteen. So there's no reason why you shouldn't bring your friends and relatives along to enjoy the subsidies. As a break during shopping, perhaps.

## Free Meals at Work

A choice way of enjoying an expensive meal at the firm's expense (while impressing colleagues) is to tell the boss you have a few productivity ideas. 'Perhaps I could pass them on over lunch, sometime.' If there's pressure from head office to improve profits, and there always is, you'll be treated at a restaurant before you can say 'free nosh'.

Put an anonymous note in the suggestion box saying morale is low. Suggest a few uplifting cocktail buffets on the premises.

If a sales representative wants an appointment, ask him to call at 12.30. He's bound to suggest buying you lunch. You'll be more familiar with the area's restaurants. So you can offer to choose the venue. Pick the most expensive.

## Company Junkets

Enlightened businesses organize cocktail buffets from time to time to keep staff and (more usually) customers happy.

While everyone else begins by accepting wine or sherry, you should ask for a large glass of mineral water. Then when refills are offered, you change to wine. Your glass will be three times bigger than the rest.

Towards the end of the affair, keep your eye on valued customers who are about to fall over. Catch them before they do, and suggest to the boss that you call a taxi at company expense to see them safely home. You get a free lift, too.

## The Tea-break

Most office and shop staff have an average six cuppas a day. Factory and outdoor workers drink even more. It's cheaper to chip in for a kettle, teapot, mugs, tea, coffee and sugar and make your own.

But if there's a tea bar, you'll be expected to buy a full round for everyone at least once a day. You can reduce this expensive chore to once a week with the 'big noise' technique.

It works like this. When you go for the tea, make a commotion about it. Sing or crack jokes as you collect the order. Pretend to trip and almost spill the lot when you come back.

In this way your contribution will be remembered. It'll seem that you do the honours more often than you do.

Tea rounds are frequently made at 10 a.m. People who missed breakfast may ask for a doughnut or scone to keep them going. Don't offer to get tea at this critical time.

Another danger point when people start to order cakes with their tea is around 4 p.m. Keep your head down then, too.

## Christmas Parties and Other Entertainments

Volunteer to organize the office 'do'. Delegate the boring jobs like blowing up balloons to office juniors who haven't grown out of this sort of thing. Then set a cover charge for drinks and nibbles. This can be quite large as it's Christmas. Don't, of course, pay the levy yourself.

Or, instead of the usual party, arrange a night at the theatre, ballet, opera or pantomime. The management will always let you in free for bringing such a large party.

On Derby Day, arrange the office sweep. It seems fair that you shouldn't have to pay for your own ticket.

## Money-saving Perks

Work for a bank or building society and your mortgage rate will be as little as five per cent. Also, you get free life insurance and a pension, without making contributions.

Marks and Spencer's assistants get free chiropody and cancer screening. Cadbury's let employees eat as many unwrapped chocolates as they like. And beauticians with Max Factor get make-up for nothing.

Other firms, including British Gas, offer cheap shares. And some concerns pay for child care.

If your company offers nothing extra – not even luncheon vouchers – it's time to lobby for change.

## Saving Money at Work

Ask the firm's bankers for a mortgage. If your company is profitable, you may get a low rate of interest as a goodwill gesture.

Find out who the company suppliers are. Then, if you want a home computer, or telephone answering machine, you can ask if your requirements can be added to the firm's order. You'll then get the same discount for bulk.

It's generally dishonest to put your own mail through the franking machine. But sometimes this is justified if your letter has some connection with your job. If your pay cheque is late, say, and you want to send it on to the bank quickly. Or if you're applying for details about a personal pension the firm doesn't provide.

Before sitting a professional examination, conspire with a colleague to drop hints to the boss to give you a bonus if you pass. Study hard, and even the tax man won't be able to touch your just reward. And any cash you might get for making a profitable suggestion to the firm is also untaxable.

Some firms lay on morning and evening papers for visitors. You can wave goodbye to newsagent bills, and keep the reception area tidy, by taking home one or two copies at the day's end.

Occasionally, proud gardeners on the staff will bring produce to the office to show off. Keep a plastic container and a carrier bag handy in your desk. This equipment is also useful to carry off wine, sandwiches and biscuits after office meetings.

Workplaces have a large floor area. Commercial carpet off-cuts are not skimpy like domestic off-cuts. They're huge. When the office has been recarpeted, ask if you can take the spare bits home. I once carpeted a whole house like this. The same goes for bathroom tiles, wallpaper and tins of paint.

If your firm has a first-aid clinic, you can save money on having inoculations, for foreign holidays perhaps, by asking the nurse if she can do them there. Gardeners should also have tetanus jabs at company expense. It is, after all, in everyone's interest that you shouldn't come down with malaria or blood poisoning.

## Ten Cunning Ways to Promotion

This will, of course, earn you more money and perks for doing less:

 Advancement is easier if you look older. Wear soberly dark clothing of traditional cut. Men should grow a beard, and put on weight. Women should look like Margaret Thatcher. Get to know the words of old hits, including music-hall favourites, to sing at office parties.

Some bosses like their executives to have a mind of their own. Most don't. Seek out your managing director's preference. Act accordingly.

Read up on the chairman's hobby, be it ferrets or opera. Then you can monopolize his conversation at company get-togethers.

Cast rivals for promotion in poor light by spreading gossip. Or leave incriminating notes on their desk – e.g.: 'Sue, a man called Sid rang. He says he's got enough computer ribbons at present, but he can sell more paper clips if you can get them.'

Keep your ears open for ideas from others. Adopt them as your own. Reproduce them in the privacy of the boss's office. Mix socially with employees from rival firms. Appropriate their ideas, too.

Keep an old jacket or shoulder-bag in a filing cupboard. Hang them over your chair when you need to slope off early. You'll be thought to be staying late instead.

Come in early occasionally. Surround yourself with empty coffee cups and full ashtrays. The boss will suppose you've been working all night.

If you're late, secrete your coat or jacket in the toilet. Then walk into the office coatless, as though you have been at work for some time. (I've heard seasoned skivers say it pays to walk in backwards as though you're just going out.)

Never invite the boss for dinner. Things could go horribly wrong. And home entertaining is sickeningly expensive.

Take a conspicuous liking to any of your employer's children who come visiting.

## The Overdue Rise

Never make an appointment to ask for a rise. Simply knock on the door. The boss won't have time to think of reasons why you don't deserve one.

If you really are valued by the firm, be seen reading the 'jobs vacant' column before you apply. Arrange for a friend to ring the boss's secretary posing as the managing director of a rival firm. Get him to ask for you.

Make your appeal in the early afternoon, towards the end of a good week. Your employer will feel more generous after a boozy lunch.

Suggest your rise in salary just before her summer break or in

Christmas week. She's more likely to be in a relaxed holiday mood then.

When requesting more money, you'll have to do most of the talking. Prepare lots of sound reasons why you should earn more. Quote a list of your achievements, or other initiatives which the boss isn't aware failed miserably.

Don't be tempted to appear in tatters to demonstrate you need the money. Companies only reward people they want to keep. They don't retain tramps.

If, however, you have a small daughter, it's useful to dress her in a patched coat. Then contrive for the boss to 'bump into' you both in the street a few days before you ask for your increase.

Remember, too, that even obvious flattery seems to work on the most astute people. Say, 'It's a pleasure to work with a firm as professionally run as this. But, when you can get a better salary with an inferior firm like Blenkinsops, for instance (an arch rival), I owe it to my family to consider my future.'

If all fails, and no more money is coming your way, suggest a few perks instead. Will the firm pay your rail fare? Will it give luncheon vouchers or arrange an interest-free car loan? You won't know unless you ask.

## Holidays

Let your holiday allowance build up. With so many days owing, ask for extra money instead. This is a double money-spinner because you won't have to pay for your holidays either.

If you have a minor illness, like a cold or tummy bug, think twice about staying off work. Besides acquiring a work-shy reputation you'll only add to your food, fuel and electricity bills, as well as hastening wear and tear in your home.

## Using Colleagues to Save Money

While spending eight hours a day with the same team, it's easy to glean who's short of money. The cleaner may well come round and 'do' your house at a cheaper rate. The firm's decorator, plumber or electrician may be similarly obliging, especially if you go out of your way to befriend them first.

Engineering staff can also be very accommodating, fanatically keen even, over mending radios and toasters. Bring them in for repair over lunchtimes and tea-breaks.

And young colleagues can fall over themselves to baby-sit for nothing, especially if you bring your progeny to the office once or twice to show it off.

## Whip-rounds

It's customary to hold a whip-round for colleagues who are retiring or moving on. Over the year, these annoying interludes build up to quite a sum.

They're particularly galling if you've been at your post for eons, and the recipient, whom you never liked, is moving on for a higher salary somewhere else.

Luckily the money is usually collected in a large envelope. It's hard to know what you put in (unless you make the mistake of contributing early on).

One trick is to delve into your purse for a concealed handful of copper. This sounds more generous than a pound coin or a £10 note going in.

I keep a tube of glue in my drawer. When a dreaded envelope comes round, I put a dab on my first and second fingers, and stick a pound coin on each. The money is clearly seen going into the envelope, but comes out again in my closed fist.

Some collection envelopes have a list of names on the side. Tick off your name, if it's left with you, but don't put anything in. Alternatively, visit the toilet if you spot the envelope going round.

Two other antidotes to the collection envelope rely on the fallibility of memory. One is to regret, 'I haven't any change for a £20 note at the moment, I'll put some money in a bit later on.' The collector will remember asking you for a contribution, but will forget that you never came back.

The other way is to wave a large note around the envelope for some time while chatting about something else. You never actually put it in. But everyone will think you did.

You can actually make money out of somebody's leaving if you try this simple ploy. Search your home for something you can't stand. A hideous oriental vase for instance.

Tell your colleagues that the leaver is a tireless collector of Chinese ceramics. 'And I've just seen a wonderful example. I just know she'd love to have it.' It will be surmised you spotted the thing in a shop window.

All you do now is accept the collection money and hand over the vase, in perfectly fair exchange. The recipient won't want to spoil her farewell speech by turning her nose up at her unlovely gift. Neither will she object to being regarded as a connoisseur of Eastern works of art.

You'll be quids in, rid of a monstrosity, and possibly revenged on someone you didn't like.

Workmates who leave often arrange celebrations in the pub on their last day. These are well worth attending as the departer normally pays for the drinks. He'll doubtless hand over a kitty to the licensee. Check with bar staff when this bounty is likely to run out. Recall your previous engagement just before it does.

## The Order of the Boot

If you're about to be sacked, let it happen. If you haughtily resign first, you'll lose rights to redundancy pay and unemployment benefit.

When a long-faced manager tells you the news, you can afford to forget your pride altogether. (After all, you won't see much of her again.)

Grasp the chair arm, quiver your lower lip, even break into tears. Babble incoherently about your mortgage and poor children. Anything to get a few months' extra pay on compassionate grounds.

## Leaving Your Job

Be exceptionally nice to colleagues the week before you go. Ask about their problems, lavish compliments, fetch cups of tea. And don't make demands on their time. This ensures a generous leaving present.

Drop hints about what you really want. Mention that your radio cassette player has blown up or your handbag has dropped to bits. Otherwise you'll end up with a useless inscribed tankard or another set of glasses.

## Organize Your Own Leaving Collection

Approach a hard-up colleague. Offer a small sum if he'll take up your goodbye collection to your instructions. Put a few £10 notes in the bottom of a generous open container – like a bucket – 'to set the pace'.

Give the conspiratorial collector another £10 note to put in himself in front of colleagues, uttering the words, 'We're all going to miss her, you know.' This is best done after lunch when a few of the donors may have been drinking.

And make sure the collector gets the widest possible circulation for contributions by visiting other departments. Even if they don't know you, they (foolish people) will not want to appear to be mean.

# Food and Drink

Spare and have is better than spend and crave.
—*Benjamin Franklin*

IN 1960, the weekly food bill amounted to a third of the family income. Now only a fifth of our income pays for what we eat. Even so, a careful buyer can do better than that. He'll save a lot of time and eat more healthily, too.

The first rule is to let others buy or cook meals for you. The second is to shop for food just once a week.

Use supermarkets and street markets. Have no truck with all that sentimentality over the decline of corner shops. If they can't be competitive, you can't afford to patronize them, sad though this may be.

A trip to the supermarket shouldn't waste petrol. A car-driving friend must be persuaded to make the weekly trip with you. Simply say that you want to turn a boring weekly chore into an interesting social occasion. She'll be too flattered to notice the baser motive. Cultivate the arrangement into a habit.

## Ten Ways to Penny-pinch at Supermarkets

 Have a bar of chocolate before taking up the trolley. A hungry shopper buys more than he needs.

Go on a Saturday, particularly before a bank holiday. You'll find plenty of bargains whose sell-by dates are still one or two days away. Also, shop in the late afternoon, when pies and cakes are drastically reduced.

Sleepy cashiers sometimes ring up reduced items at normal prices. Watch the till and check your receipt.

Buy in bulk. Not only is this cheaper in the long run, it saves shopping time. And bigger cartons and packets give your kitchen an opulent look.

Don't fall for gimmicks, like special spoons for taking cat food out of tins, and other dubiously useful kitchen gadgets.

Look for damaged packets, split bags and tins which have lost labels. Reduced cans with dents in them are safe. Beware of damaged seams though. And bulges in the can means something inside is definitely off.

Buy the supermarket's own brand. The contents taste the same – and very often are the same – as brands with 'household names'.

Before you reach out for some attractive morsel, ask yourself if you're only tempted because it was advertised on TV last night.

Don't buy fruit and veg in supermarkets. It's cheaper and often fresher on market stalls.

Wear tight trousers when touring a supermarket – to remind you of your diet.

## Ten More Ways to Penny-pinch at Supermarkets

 Don't take grasping children with you.

Stick to a list. It helps avoid the psychological traps they use to shift items nobody wants.

Be adventurous. If you see something you wouldn't normally eat, but it's dramatically reduced, give it a try.

Don't buy those household management magazines you see strategically placed near the checkout. Read them as you wait your turn.

The larger the store, the bigger the discounts.

Know the loss leaders – the bargains supermarkets advertise in the press and chalk on their windows to get more punters in.

Supermarkets are now stuffed with exotic fruits like kiwis, star fruit, babacos, kumquats, pepinos and tamarillos. Tell the manager you've never heard of two or three of these and would he give you a free sample to see if you like them. But never buy them. They cost more than they're worth because of shipping costs.

Be unseasonal. All right, Christmas puddings may be unthinkable after the event, but lots of fruit cake and biscuits only become Christmas items because of robins and holly on the box. They're sold at giveaway prices in January. And egg-shaped chocolate is still chocolate after Easter.

Push aside items at the front of shelves and feel around towards the back. Because of inflation, tins and boxes that have been there longer may be labelled more cheaply than those at the front.

Food sold loose is cheaper than food sold in bags which is cheaper than food in rigid containers.

You need every one of those tips. Superstore managers are trained in pop psychology to make you spend, spend, spend. If you're aware of these dirty tricks, you won't fall for them.

## The Supermarket Racket

The moment you walk through the doors, you're given a false first impression. Indoor plants, loose fruit and vegetables are put near the entrance to make you think everything is fresh and wholesome. In fact, most wares are dried, tinned, preserved and frozen.

Heavy goods go to the front of the store, so you take a trolley, instead of a basket. You're then tempted to pile in extra items. These trolleys are getting bigger all the time, so that they nearly always appear half empty.

Things we all need like bread, margarine and milk are at the back of the store so we have to pass loads of tempting luxuries to get to them. These basic items are always split up: we can't just go to one section of the store and walk out.

Nobody resists the smell of hot bread. So bakeries are put at the back. We're then drawn right into the store. Some supermarkets don't even make bread, they simply heat up the loaves to get the homely smell.

Things that are easy to sell, including sugar and soap powder, are put on the lowest shelves. When we straighten up we come face to face with expensive goods strategically displayed at eye-level. These basic items are usually split – and their positions are often changed around – so we have to hunt round to find them.

Deceptive lighting is everywhere. Pink bulbs make meat look juicy. Green lights make vegetables look fresher.

Shelves are sometimes left half empty to make us think some items are so desirable, there's been a run to buy them. Rival brands are moved away from each other to stop us comparing prices.

Expensive luxury goods are put at the end of aisles. That's when we slow up our trollies to take corners, and have more time to look.

Gimmicky gadgets are often placed around the food. New-fangled can-openers go near the tins, fancy bottle openers by the wine, and party poppers next to the crisps. Sweets and children's books go near the check-out where parents – now exhausted by trailing round the store – are too tired to resist bored children who pick them up.

## The Supermarket Alternative

Start your own bulk-buying co-operative with eight friends and neighbours. One person makes a weekly trip to the wholesale food market or nearby market garden and buys mountainous quantities. Divide it all up later.

The task will only fall to you six times a year. Or not at all, if you set yourself up as organizer. Or you could make sure your car has 'just broken down' as your turn looms.

It's also tempting to befriend any food retailer who has one of those cards which allow entry to a cash-and-carry warehouse. This is where traders only can buy in bulk at wholesale prices. But beware!

The Federation of Wholesale Distributors say that any trader lending out his card, or using it to supply friends, is breaking a sacred trust. And though he's not acting illegally, he could be banned from all cash-and-carry warehouses for a long time. Culprits, says the Federation, are quickly found out.

## Street Markets

Always go to markets just before 5 p.m. on a Saturday. By then, traders who may not be back in business for another week are trying to give the stuff away. Very often, they do just that.

Stall holders are famed for their warm hearts, so if one gives you a bargain, it's worth saying 'You're so kind, that really helps when you're on a pension', or 'Thanks, the money doesn't go far, does it, when you've got six kids?'

He'll take it that these general statements apply to you, and will shower you with free food.

It's not uncommon to find the occasional box of apples or cabbages abandoned on the pavement. If you've reason to believe a trader intended to dispose of it, you can legally help yourself.

But, as picking up food in the street isn't normally favoured by persons of quality, it's best to wear dark glasses, or ask your children to do this.

It was once plausibly argued by a friend of mine that if one could elegantly spear fruit and veg on a pointed stick with a silver top, picking up produce from the street would be socially acceptable. He made one, and has never looked back.

The nearer the fruit was grown to home the better the bargain. There'll be no shipping bills for the wholesaler to add on. Kiwi fruit, tangerines and limes should take second place to apples and pears.

Environmental Health Officers sometimes warn that food other than fresh fruit and veg, sold on market stalls, may be less than wholesome.

But tinned food lasts a long, long time, biscuits and cakes sometimes improve with keeping, and jars of coffee, tea-bags and pop –

staple commodities on market stalls – don't go off easily.

Use-by dates may come and go, but these are usually on the conservative side. Buying from cut-rate market stalls is using your eyes and common sense.

In any event, cut-price food traders stand in the same spot for years. Any one case of food poisoning would force market authorities to send them packing straight away.

## Other Ways to Fill Larders

Tasty home-made cakes, pastries and jam can be bought from smiling matrons at car boot sales, church bazaars and summer fetes. Not only are these goodies cheap, but you won't find the usual commercial chemicals interfering with both taste and health.

The wholesome way to buy potatoes, eggs and honey is at local farms. Collect them on your way to somewhere else, to make the saving worth the petrol.

But another farm enterprise, picking your own fruit, isn't worth the bother. You'll end up paying for more than you really want. You could also put your back out.

And do away with your milkman (not literally of course). His doorstep leavings tend to mount up, unused, in the fridge. Like his weekly bill.

Take advantage of those excellent shops which provide scoops so you can buy dried or frozen foods by weight. Everything's cheaper because there are no brand names to advertise at your expense. Shopping here is socially desirable, too, because there's none of the kind of overpackaging which sees off rain forests.

## How to Get Free Food

When a new food comes on the market, write off for a free sample. Do this even though it's not offered in the advertising. If they haven't made a trial size, you'll be sent a full-sized sample instead.

Don't enclose return postage. They'll be grateful enough that somebody is taking an interest in a product yet to prove itself.

They'll only expect to send one sample per household. But you can write care of friends and relatives, too. Use your name, without the initials. Then, after a week or so, ask the different addressees if there's been any mail for you.

You can also keep yourself in free toothpaste and detergents in exactly the same way.

Another profitable dodge involves going into any disreputable-looking shop for a small box of chocolates. Pick one at the back of the very top shelf.

If any of the contents is mouldy, send them back to the manufacturers. They'll post you a huge selection of their wares to keep your goodwill.

Always send faulty goods back, however slight the imperfection. Examples: 'The nuts in your fruit-and-nut chocolate are too hard', or, 'The colour of this strawberry jelly isn't quite red enough.'

Complain to the manufacturer, never the shop, and you'll get a return parcel worth ten times as much.

One of my most profitable occupations is to weigh the contents of food cartons on the kitchen scales. If they're well below the weight on the packet, back they go to the makers for another wide selection of their products.

Now, what happens if you buy a box of Crispy Crunch cereal with the free offer of a plastic dinosaur inside, and it isn't there? Well, you can eat all the cereal, then return to the shop and demand *all* they promised. As they're not likely to have a spare brontosaur hanging around, you're legally entitled to another boxful. With a bit of luck that will be monsterless, too. And so it could go on.

The more prestigious the store, the more likely it is that food tasting will be going on. Harrods is a good example. Don't be shy to take advantage, especially on lunch-time shopping trips.

Cheese factories, breweries and cider makers nearly always provide a similar bounty. Write to the public relations officer for details.

Tell major food manufacturers that you enjoy their products and would like to help their market research into any new lines. You could be deluged with samples.

You could also remind an elderly relative of her legendary skills of making home-made jams and chutney. Suggest she takes up the hobby again. Hint that she may have lost her touch. Perhaps she may prove you wrong.

If you've an appealing small child, send her into the greengrocers to make a heart-rending plea: 'Have you got any spare carrots, please, for Flopsie the Rabbit?' Flopsie the Rabbit, of course, being the nickname she has for you. Well, it all helps!

## Money-saving Offers

It's not worth bothering with money-off coupons, unless utterly desperate. True, some shops make it more worthwhile by accepting coupons for another firm's products, but that's blatantly dishonest.

So let's hurry on to a trick practised by manufacturers which is just as questionable.

On offer is a picture card or tacky plastic car inside a box of cereal, say. One of the set will be very rare. Your children will pester you to keep buying the stuff, long after everyone's sick of it, just to get this elusive prize. Of course, it never does fall onto the breakfast table.

The dilemma is solved by writing to the firm: 'I have bought dozens of packets of your excellent product, but have yet to get the spotted gnat lark. For the sake of a little boy who cries himself to sleep each night, please help.'

A full set of picture cards will arrive by return post. You'll also get a gilded album, together with a selection of the firms' products, if you add in your letter: 'And even the Trading Standards Officer is becoming interested in young Simon's plight.'

Now here's a super dodge. Sometimes firms will offer a coupon on a carton of pizza, say, entitling buyers to another pizza free. Take the meal home and eat it. Return with the coupon. When the assistant hands over your free carton, tear off your new coupon before his eyes, and ask for another pizza. Keep going until you've been given the entire stock.

The shop has to play ball to stay within the law, as an enterprising solicitor found recently when he successfully put this ploy to the test.

## Tips on Making Food Go Further

 When making cakes, add less sugar and eggs than advised in the recipe. It tastes exactly the same.

Dilute fruit juice by one-third tap water. You'll hardly notice. And water down canned soup, adding a little potato powder to rethicken it.

Over-ripe bananas are gloriously cheap. Mash them into a tasty sandwich spread.

Use loose tea. It's half the price of tea bags and tastes better. Using a teapot is stylish anyway.

If you discover a cheap meal, but the kids hate it, rename it Space Stew or Rambo's Delight. It will become a regular favourite.

Rice can be served instead of potatoes nearly every time. It's cheaper to buy and quicker to cook.

Make constant remarks about bulging waist-lines to members of the family.

That sudden urge to have a cup of tea or coffee could be old-fashioned thirst. Have a glass of water instead.

Wean yourself off sugar addiction by gradually taking less in tea and coffee. This will help you to cut out expensive chocolate bars, sweets and fizzy drinks.

The human nervous system isn't capable of grabbing a saucepan before milk starts to boil over. But the process can be stopped in its tracks by giving the base a hefty whack on the cooker top.

## Making Your Drinks Cupboard Go Further

 Rum and gin can be slightly watered with little effect, but whisky tends to take on a tell-tale cloudiness.

Funnel cheap sherry and port into decanters. They taste better immediately.

Decant a poor-quality whisky into a bottle which once contained a rare malt, to impress less-discerning friends. This also works for gin, port and sherry.

After offering your guests coffee laced with whisky or rum, add artificial flavourings instead. You can buy them for a few pence from the supermarket.

When carrying out a small favour for someone, casually reveal your favourite tipple. You may be rewarded with a bottle.

## Hoarding

It's worth squirrelling away tinned and dried foods. Running out of something to eat means a hurried visit to an expensive small shop. Or worse, you might desperately order take-aways – a financial disaster for anyone with a family.

## The Ice-cream Menace

Ice-cream and lollies are an unwarranted expense when those infernal chiming vans come round. Keep a sharp ear open, especially on Sunday afternoons, and turn up the television at the first sign of this nuisance.

If an ice-cream seller makes a regular visit to your street, adopt a 'favourite' radio programme at the same time. Play it loud to drown the chimes.

Ice-cream can be made quite cheaply by lacing evaporated milk with sugar and flavouring.

## Growing your Own

Producing your food from your soil isn't as arduous as many cynics think. And the savings on fruit, vegetables and shopping trips will swell any bank balance.

Organic food is particularly pricey. But your own stuff can be as organic as you like. Simply stop buying fertilizing chemicals in favour of the contents of your compost heap. Home-grown food is also utterly fresh: you've just picked it.

If your garden is small or non-existent, you don't have to be a little old man to rent an allotment for next to nothing. And you can use grow-bags or even window boxes.

There are no rules against growing vegetables next to flowers. You can also save space by putting quick-growing radishes very near to potatoes or parsnips. The radishes will be ready in four to six weeks: before their neighbours take all the space.

Anyway this isn't a gardener's book, but a manual for people who want to live in luxury without spending money. So all I'll say is that potatoes, runner beans, onions, lettuce, marrows, parsnips, courgettes, carrots and pumpkins are the easiest things in the world to grow.

Buy a book on it. Better still, put a row of seeds in the ground, and hope for the best.

And if some of your crops fail, you can eke out the salad with washed dandelion leaves.

## Storing Food

Buy a big second-hand freezer. Don't pay a lot, as the market is flooded with people moving to smaller homes with nowhere to put them. Keep it in a chilly cellar or garage to halve running costs.

Freezers are ideal for home-grown vegetables, bulk-buying and for serving leftovers, weeks after the original meal.

If you haven't got cold storage, potatoes, carrots and swedes can be left in cardboard boxes in layers with sand packed in between. Store in the dark. Keep tomatoes wrapped in newspapers in drawers where they'll ripen very slowly. Hang onions in a string bag in the kitchen, for that fashionable rustic look.

When guests have gone, remove the fruit bowl and put it somewhere cold and drab where the contents will keep much longer.

May I now entertain you with some of the crazier tips about food storage?

Eggs keep longer with the round end upwards.

Four cubes of sugar in a tin of biscuits will keep the contents crisp.

Carrots last twice as long with the tops cut off.

## Growing Your Own Fruit

A real healthy money-saver this. All kinds of fruit can easily be planted and hardly ever tended: brambles, gooseberries, raspberries, rhubarb, bilberries, strawberries. Apple, pear and plum trees are well worth their keep. But be prepared for disappointment with cherries, peaches and figs.

Be sceptical about some of those newspaper ads which offer wonder fruit trees, bearing oodles of exotic fruit, merely by buying a miniature bush for the patio.

## How to Get Free Fruit

In the good old days, one could lurk around ne'er-do-wells in the stocks, to gather up any undamaged fruit used as avenging missiles on the village green. Nowadays, a little more subtlety is called for.

Gallantly volunteer to pick fruit for elderly neighbours who find apples and pears too high to reach. They'll gratefully pass the surplus on.

Or lean over the garden fence and confide to your neighbour, 'Your plums are in super condition. Wish I had green fingers like that!' You'll proudly be offered a bagful forthwith.

When calling on friends, it's always acceptable to ask for something from the fruit bowl. It is, of course, quite different from requesting something in your host's larder.

## Wine and Beer

Veer away from wine boxes. They may work out cheaper in terms of quantity, but they encourage drinking at every meal. You'll seem more extravagant by occasionally opening a bottle.

Making your own wine is tricky. Only do it if you have the patience. Beer is different. Home brewing hardly ever goes wrong. And the result, unlike do-it-yourself wine, is actually tastier and stronger than the commercial variety. Ordinary kitchen equipment is all you need.

## Fooling Visitors into Thinking You're a Wealthy Gourmet

Nonchalantly ask guests if they would like some caviar. Serve them with fish paste on toast. Don't fret. Even if they have tried the real thing before, they'll have forgotten its subtle flavour.

Have some obscure cookbooks lying around the kitchen table, like 'Cooking with Icelandic Herbs' or '100 Ways to Serve Etruscan Delicacies'. No need to buy them. Simply put a brown paper cover on any paperback and boldly ink in the title with a fluorescent green pen.

There's no need to buy exotic teas. Add a blackcurrant leaf from the garden to the cheapest tea. It will give it a luxurious flavour.

## The Ultimate Tip

Cut down on your food bill by going on a diet. Official statistics tell me you're probably overweight.

# Personal Spending

Get what you can, and what you get hold;
'Tis the stone that will turn all your lead into gold.
—*Benjamin Franklin*

THERE'S this barmy tendency for people of wealthier nations, like Britain, to entertain ourselves by going shopping. That's why so many useless gimmicks are sold . . . not as necessities, but amusements. The solution: don't go near a store unless you absolutely have to buy something.

You can avoid shops and have lots of fun 'treasure-hunting' if you buy everything, except food, second time round. Generally speaking, the older your purchase, the more it will appreciate in value. Try selling something new for more than you paid!

## Furniture

New furniture is both expensive and, often, fairly shoddy. And, as most pleasing designs have been thought of by now, a great deal of better-quality contemporary furniture apes period style anyway.

Such reproductions are usually more expensive than original Victorian, or even Georgian furniture, so you might as well try for a genuinely antique table or set of chairs.

Older relatives, moving from family homes into bungalows, are a reliable source of furniture and household paraphernalia. All you need do is put it on the family grapevine that you're short of stuff.

Also worth a go is the 'I do like that' tactic. When visiting the target gushily exclaim, 'Ooh, I do love that little chair in the hall. I wish I had something like that for the bedroom.' It's best to single out something not too valuable, otherwise you could appear avaricious.

Antique shops are expensive places to buy furniture. And years of browsing through junk shops hasn't revealed to me one presentable piece of period furniture. The only place to buy decent stuff is at modest salerooms (see the chapter on How to Buy at Auctions).

There's nothing more effective than cheap, fragile, lopsided, wobbly furnishings to make you look poverty-stricken. But nasty pieces can be disguised in several ways to give a convincing, luxurious look.

Tables, both square and circular, can be covered to the floor with

floral or lace cloths. You can even make a tea chest, with a circle of plywood nailed on top, look good like that.

Beds which have lost a leg can be balanced on breeze blocks, with a valance to hide the imperfection. Unstable chairs can be propped against a wall, with permanent knitting on the seat, to stop people sitting on them.

Most people know the trick of taking old floorboards from a skip and stacking them on house bricks to use as a bookcase. Fine – if you want to look impoverished. But you can improvise a more respectable bookcase if you put book jackets round the bricks. Then the shelving will look attached to the wall.

## Bric-a-brac

Old ornaments, with cracks and lumps missing, cost very little. If you stand these same antiques with their imperfections against a wall, they'll appear to be perfect. Glaring chips in the rim of a vase can be covered over with artistically drooping flowers.

As visitors will never be so rude as to inspect your effects with an eagle eye, you can get away with all sorts of botched repairs. This will save the huge fees demanded by professional restorers.

My home is filled with expensive-looking antiques, nearly all heavily damaged. Given the right location, under soft lighting, it's hard to spot the repairs, even when you know they're there.

Once football hooligans kicked to bits a large art nouveau jug I was transporting by train. The pieces were later stuck together like a jigsaw. Apart from some unusually heavy crazing, it passes as perfect again.

A child's set of watercolours can disguise chips in pottery; a pot of gold paint touches up gilt picture frames, a brown wax crayon sees off scratches in furniture. Big holes in almost anything can be filled with a mixture of Polyfilla and turps substitute.

I recently bought a Georgian circular mirror dirt cheap because three or four tiny gilt spheres around the frame were missing. I stuck gob-stoppers in their place, covered in gold paint.

Don't fret. This kind of repair won't detract from an already reduced value. But it will gentrify your home.

## Paintings

Nothing enhances financial status as much as a fine art collection. Happily, third-rate watercolours and oils can be mistaken for top-notch work if you hang them high up on walls in dark corners.

Poor oil paintings which are damaged are often given away, but holes can be obliterated by putting sticking plaster behind the canvas and smearing over with boot polish.

To the untrained eye, the worst of daubs can look like an important work of art, if it's well mounted and framed. So look out for old frames. Don't worry if they look battered. Some of the world's most distinguished pictures have ropey frames. It's part of their mystique.

Or you can execute your own 'abstract painting' with a few tubes of oil paint made in Taiwan. It won't actually look like the work of a four-year-old, if you frame it. And you can truthfully describe it to friends as a picture from the 'primitive school'.

## Mirrors

These are essential for making rooms appear bigger. But if you come across one with a poor reflecting surface, think twice before having the glass replaced. Very old (and consequently, valuable) mirrors are difficult to see into. Putting in modern glass attacks their value.

You can tell old mirror glass by putting a pencil point to the surface. If the lead and its reflection touch, then it's period glass. If there's a gap, it's modern.

Ornate picture frames can be turned into mirrors quite cheaply by taking them to a glazier and asking him to put in reflective glass. It's done while you wait.

## High-street Shopping

Bargains aren't only to be found during the January sales. For instance, if a TV set is the last model in the range, it will be sold off very cheaply indeed. I got £200 off mine.

And all electrical goods are sold for ridiculous prices if they're not all there. My video was half price, because the instruction book was missing and the remote control doofa couldn't be found. I managed to buy the missing bit for £10 on a market stall – though, to be honest, I still haven't mastered the video.

Deal in cash, not credit cards, and you can bargain at least ten per cent off most large items (ironically known as consumer durables, though they often don't last very long). This is because managers of chain stores are subject to heavy pressure to keep their weekly takings up. If you've already waved notes in front of them, they get very panicky if you make moves to leave without buying anything after all.

## A Colour TV for the Price of Black-and-white

Not only can you transform a cheap black-and-white set, but you won't have to pay for a colour licence either. Cut a piece of perspex to the size of the screen. With photographic tints from an art shop, lightly paint the middle section pink. Then colour a narrower strip in green (for grass) at the bottom and another strip in blue (for the sky) at the top. Stick it to the screen with clear tape.

Naturally this filter works best for outside programmes, but interiors look more interesting, too.

## Lastly . . .

May I add a final tip which works for all kinds of shopping, but particularly when buying spare parts, DIY items and antiques: simply ask the general question, on behalf of the world in general, 'How much off for trade?'

# A Better Place of Your Own

Live with a thrifty, not a needy fate;
Small shots paid often waste a vast estate.
—*Robert Herrick*

IF you follow advice in this book, you'll soon be able to afford a better home. But if it's bigger, there'll be heavier spending on maintenance, decorating, heating, carpeting and garden plants. If it's further away from work, schools and shops, it will mean more petrol and bus fares. Bad news.

But, unless your family is spreading, your abode doesn't have to be big and remote to fit your blossoming status. Simply move into the smartest part of town. A penthouse overlooking the river, perhaps, or a sixteenth-century timber-framed job. Something unusual will always sell when you decide to move on.

If your new home falls just outside the very best area, don't let that stop you including this desirable district in your address. Enough people in your street will be doing this for the postman not to get confused.

It's the same old story. If you exhibit the trappings of social success – and a smart address is among the best of these – opportunities grow on trees.

## Selling Your Old House

Confide in two estate agents that you want to sell your home. Keen for the business, they'll be round with their tape measures before you've time to explain you don't need *them* to sell it. Ask for their valuations, but don't commit yourself.

If they telephone later, put them off by saying, 'I'm sorry, I'm not ready to sell through you yet. Something has come up.' (This could be a tulip in the garden.)

Using their estimates as a guide, advertise your home in the paper. Don't lose your nerve over doing this every week. You'll spend a lot less than an agent's commission.

If you can find a copy of the agent's blurb when you bought the house, use that to produce your own set of details. 'For Sale' signs can be bought at stationers.

If any neighbours are also selling up, it's as good as having your home's details in *their* estate agent's window. Their callers will spot your 'For Sale' signs too.

Read the local news to see if any large factories or government departments are setting up nearby. Send a set of details to the personnel officer.

## Taking Advantage of an Estate Agent

If you fail to sell privately, you'll eventually have to resort to an agent. The rate of commission rarely varies, so you might as well choose the firm with the most prominent office – in the town centre or near the railway station.

Use more than one, and you'll pay extra commission. This isn't worth it, as serious buyers will check every agent in the area.

Younger agents are more energetic than older ones. They might not be as worldly-wise, but experience doesn't really count in their business. There isn't a lot to learn.

Should the firm prove sloppy and lethargic, and no one remembers your face when you call, rapidly ditch them for another agency. Check your contract first for that vital 'no sale, no fee' clause.

If they sell your home very quickly, before their advertising costs have built up, it's fair to argue that there wasn't time to give you the full service. So try sending only half the fee.

An accompanying letter should read, 'Though I'm grateful, perhaps you'll agree that paying thousands of pounds for just a few days' work is a little unreasonable.' You could also hint that their valuation must have been off beam (which it probably was).

Estate agents are trained to be nice to people, and may not press you for the rest.

## Sneaky Ways to Force a Sale

 Don't invite people between eight and ten in the morning, and between four and six at night, when the road outside is busiest.

It's said every vase of cut flowers (from the garden) adds one thousand pounds to the value of the house. The smell of baking has also sold thousands of houses. So keep a piece of dough ready to put in the oven.

Inform callers you were told by the previous owner that a hoard of oil paintings may be in the loft. You're frightened of spiders and have never been up there.

Arrange for a friendly neighbour to keep an eye on your front door. As potential buyers arrive, he should phone you every three minutes. You loudly answer, 'We're showing a lot of people round tonight. Can you make it tomorrow?' Your flesh-and-blood callers will assume the house is highly desirable.

Explain that the area is pretty select because a judge and an MP live nearby. The judge could be the main man at the local ferret show, and the MP a mangey parrot.

Discover what your next-door-neighbour does for a living. Give prospective buyers a glamorous version of that occupation. If she works at a lemonade factory say she is something big in the pop world. Perhaps another resident has a familiar name. If 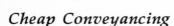 there's a Roger Moore or a Liz Taylor living nearby, you should say so.

## Cheap Conveyancing

You can do your own conveyancing for the price of a good book. Expensive lawyers can also be left out of house transfers by using a conveyancing firm. Sometimes they're very cheap, sometimes not.

Try your own conveyancing if your house is freehold, if it's much like any other, and has no onerous conditions – like rights of way.

Remember that solicitors for the party you're selling to, and lawyers for those you're buying from, won't want the sale to founder. They'll *have* to help you out if you get stuck.

Only consider a solicitor who's a relative, a friend or a friend's relative. As there's so little to conveyancing, they might work for nothing. It doesn't matter if they're based in a strange town. Completion is made by fax and telephone.

If you do get a stiff solicitor's bill, request that it's 'taxed'. This means the Law Society has to check it's fair. The outcome is seldom in doubt, of course, but at least the inevitable delay buys you time. And interest on the money.

## Buying a House

When you've found your new home, slice a reasonable amount from the asking price, in your mind. Then knock another two or three thousand off, before making your offer. You never know. There are some dozy people around, for whom money means nothing. Your silly offer might just be accepted.

Your building society will want the house inspected. Three kinds of survey will be offered – expensive, very expensive, and ridiculous. You must make your own mind up, but I always choose the cheapest inspection for three reasons:

The surveyor gets a lot of business from this building society. He won't want to queer his pitch by making any mistakes – even on the cheapest survey.

Surveyors like to imply they aren't legally responsible if a cheap survey isn't stringent enough to reveal all the faults – like a case of dry rot. Court cases have proved them wrong.

If you pay for the dearest survey, you may find it just as difficult to make the surveyor admit a mistake as he would with the least costly one.

## Second-hand Surveys

Sometimes a family will bid for a house and have a survey done. The report is a glowing one. But the family can't sell their old home, so drop out. You hear about this survey from the seller, and offer to buy it at half price to save money on having your own survey done.

This may sound like a good idea, but is it? If it's later discovered your house is sinking into the ground, the crafty surveyor will disclaim responsibility. You were never his client. Someone else was. So you can't sue.

## No Guarantee

Your new abode may need a fresh roof, or other repairs, before the building society will lend on it. The builders may offer a ten-year guarantee on this work. They may also intend to liquidate, and set up another firm offering the same service in the office next door. It's called the 'Change the Name and do the Same Game'. This makes their old guarantees worthless.

You should ask for a discount on your repairs instead of getting a long guarantee. Wait till the job's done, though, before you barter.

## A Top Tax Tip

If you follow all the sneaky secrets in this volume, you could soon have two homes. If you later decide to sell the one which isn't your main residence, you'll have to pay capital gains tax on your profit. This sum can be reduced by asking your buyer to pay more for curtains and carpets, and less for the house.

## Moving In

Large well-known removal firms have a mysterious need for new lorries, radio contact, hi-tech storage facilities, lots of computer hardware back at the office, and glossy brochures. They advertise a lot. And they need to charge VAT. Guess who pays for all this?

Let's start with the cheapest alternative — a hired van and a little help from one's friends. It's surprising how many naïve amateurs see moving furniture as a fun day out. Especially if they haven't done it lately.

No special licence is needed to drive a large van of up to three tons. Of course, more than one trip may be necessary. But on the bright side, the driving makes a convenient break from lugging wardrobes and beds about.

Your unpaid team will get jaded and bad-tempered as the day goes on. So it's wise to get everything boxed and ready beforehand. Have packed lunches laid on. The traditional moving-day visit to the fish and chip shop takes time and money.

Friends aren't always daft enough to assume removal duties, so you may have to find a 'man and van' instead. They advertise in shop windows. Ask for evidence that the vehicle is insured, taxed and MOT tested.

Insurance for your goods may be out of the question (saving a few bob). But your man will have been battered senseless long ago if he makes a habit of dropping things in driveways.

Anyway it's better to sacrifice a few bits and bobs you're probably fed up with, than to argue endlessly over whether it was covered for damages later. You can, after all, dock the miscreant's fee for any breakages.

You'll be charged by the hour, so work out the shortest, most jam-free route possible to your new home. Don't slow down the hired help by offering tea and cakes. And work as fast as you can to show an example. At the end of a busy day, resist any temptation you might have towards tipping.

## A Money-making Move

Fixtures and fittings must stay in your old home (more's the pity), but don't abandon anything else just because you don't want it. A postcard at the corner shop or a free 'under £20' insert in the newspaper will soon shift curtains, carpets and surplus furniture. So take them with you.

Don't baulk at loading the contents of the coal bunker or woodpile into buckets to take with you as well.

If there's doubt as to whether something is a fixture or not, take it. Nobody sues over trivialities. The purchasers may well grumble, but you'll probably never see them again.

It's useful to say to the vendor of your new home, 'Leave anything you want. I'll see that it's taken away.' You might get all sorts of goodies to sell in the 'for sale' columns.

## Buying a Flat

Think twice before buying a leasehold flat. You can't control the maintenance costs. You won't be able to shop around for the cheapest roofer or decorator. The leaseholders will set the service charge.

This appalling lack of opportunity to control costs could drive a careful spender like you right round the bend.

If you're already stuck with such a flat, offer to buy the leaseholder out. About ten times the annual rent would be a good bargain on your part. Your home's value will then shoot up.

## Renting

Think of it! Resolve to rent a home for the rest of your life, and you'll never be stuck with mortgage and maintenance costs. It's one of the cheapest ways to live. The only obvious snag is that you'll have no home to leave in your will – but if your dependants read this manual, they'll be rich anyway.

Retired people should certainly think about selling their home to live in a smaller rented flat. Ignore any veiled protests from immediate family, hoping to inherit, and think of all that lovely interest from the building society.

## Lovely Housing Associations

Registering with a housing association is signing up for a pot of gold. Rents are low, standards high. And after a few years, they'll usually sell you the home for a fraction of the market price.

## Free Accommodation

One way of paying no rent is to move in with relatives or a friend of the family, preferably of the same age. Write to this fortunate person saying you are starting a new job, or looking for work in her area.

'Do you know somewhere I can stay for the time being? I've tried everywhere, but it's hopeless. I know you can help me, if anyone can.' Her spare room is as good as yours.

Relatives have two advantages over ordinary lodgers: (a) they're not expected to pay market rents; (b) it's not done to force them out if they stay too long.

## Being a Lodger

Answering an advertisement for someone to share a house is *the* way of living cheaply. You may have to share gas, electricity and phone bills, as well as paying the weekly rent, but that's all.

You won't have to buy a TV, a TV licence, a washing machine, a drier, a toaster, an iron or an ironing board. Someone else will maintain the roof, lag the pipes, pay for house insurance and get plants for the garden. You won't have to supply toilet rolls, washing-up liquid, bath cleaners or flea powder for the cat.

You have a ready-made excuse for not returning the compliment of people who invite you to dinner parties. You won't be able to put up relatives.

Yes, being a lodger is highly recommended – a saver's paradise. You can even decorate your room to your own taste, and save money. Ask the landlord to knock off a few weeks' rent to pay for your labour. He should stand you the materials, of course.

Some landlords expect compensation for breakages. The trick is to admit to the first accident. Then it will be assumed you'll always do the right thing. You won't be suspected of being the culprit for the rest of the stuff you smash.

## Taking in Lodgers

This makes money but, unless you choose the right sort of paying guest, life can be hell. The ideal person is wedded to work and devoted to parents. This means they're usually at work or somewhere else they regard as their real home.

Being happy in their job ensures a steady income (to pay the rent with) and little time to socialize with friends who might otherwise clutter up your home.

Lodgers save money, too. You can read their Sunday papers and books, borrow their radios and share their tea. You won't need to decorate their room to the same standard as the rest of your home, because none of your friends will go in there.

Electricians, plumbers and engineers make excellent tenants for that odd repair job. Keen gardeners are equally useful.

It pays to suss out your lodgers' habits. You can cut down on fuel bills by using the oven or the washing machine when they do, and by making cups of tea at the same time.

But at the risk of sounding xenophobic, beware of foreign guests. They may be more interesting – but just watch your telephone bill!

# Household Bills

It was said of old Sarah, Duchess of Marlborough, that she never puts dots over her *i*'s, to save ink.

*—Horace Walpole*

IF you want to save on heating your home you must: (a) use less heat; and (b) make sure your heat isn't wasted. You can comfortably do (a) by wearing more clothing, like thicker sweaters and thermal underwear, and heating fewer rooms. It's even more effective to spend more time at friends' homes: socializing, baby-sitting and so on.

Advice on insulation is available in boring booklets from the Government, councils, and electricity and gas companies. Some of this counsel presupposes that you're skint and don't mind shivering away the winter. The following advice, in the spirit of this book, is for people who want to spend less on heating, while still living in luxury.

## Central Heating

You'll be comfortable at 65 degrees if you wear thick woolly jumpers (a mode of casual dress associated with an aristocracy used to pacing draughty baronial halls). Turn down your thermostat by just one degree centigrade and you reduce the bill by eight per cent.

Why use radiators in bedrooms when you can keep warm in bed by putting extra blankets on? You won't be pacing around all night. Switch off all central heating an hour before going to bed. Fit thermostats on radiators.

Don't rely on central heating for your main source of heat in the living room. Use a gas or open fire for that.

## Open Fires

Foster the habit of bringing home waste wood when you pass builders' skips. Bits sawed from joists and floorboards give off a lot of heat. Jump up and down on longer planks in the garden to break them into fire-sized chunks.

I once warmed myself through an entire winter by using wood begged from nearby contractors who were turning houses into flats. Council demolition sites are another supply of wood chunks, but ask permission first.

Watch out for wood which seems to be breaking down into cubes. That's dry rot. It will have been killed, however, if there has been a hard frost.

You can also get cheap machines for transforming newspapers into fuel. Or do it by hand, by pressing soggy newspaper into balls and letting it dry. Paper logs last a surprisingly long time.

Don't buy those silly little bags of coal from shops and garages. Old-fashioned deliveries give more for your money. Save by using large logs and judge things so they smoulder out just before you go up to bed.

Firelighters aren't as cheap as they look. Try newspaper rolled into tight tubes and tied into knots.

## Electricity

Electric power should be treated with respect: it's expensive. Lights are worth switching on and off. Keep a 'shock box' and fine members of the family who accidentally leave them on. Fluorescent tubes give four times the light of filament bulbs for less electricity. Keep bulbs free of dust.

Swop your electric blanket for a thermal blanket, which doesn't plug in. I'm also convinced that hundreds of thousands of pounds are wasted every year because we all fill our kettles to the top when brewing one cup of tea. Put tops on saucepans to conserve heat.

Have nothing to do with electric fires. And gas cookers are more economical than electric ones in the sense that electric hobs are still hot after you've taken the pan off.

## Gas

Gas cookers have more controllable heat. Make sure your pans are the correct size for the hobs. Adjust the flame to stay under the pan, not to envelop the sides. While the cooker's hot, use the same energy to make extra pies and cakes to eat later on.

## Home Insulation

Everyone knows that they should insulate the loft and lag the hot water tank. The trouble is the automatic grants to do this chore have now been abolished. However, the Energy Action Grants Agency may still give you the readies if you have a good sob story to tell. Write to PO Box 1NG, Newcastle-upon-Tyne, NE99 1NG.

## Wash Day

Use only half the powder or liquid recommended by the makers, who are trying to sell as much as they can.

Switch off the power-hungry tumble-dryer halfway through the programme. Leave clothes where they are for an hour. The warmth inside will finish the job.

## Ten Ways of Cutting Telephone Bills

 Resolve that your phone is mainly for incoming calls. Dial out only when you have to. And then only at weekends or after 6 p.m.

Answering machines are a boon for money-savers: other people's that is. Make the call when you know your friend is likely to be at work or shopping. Leave a message on the tape asking her to return your call.

Another good gambit is to ring in the middle of favourite TV programmes. An offer will be made to ring you back after the show.

Or you could ring someone up, only to say almost immediately, 'Oh dear, my solicitor's at the door, can you ring me back in half an hour?'

Any long-distance calls should be made from the nearest phone box. Put the minimum amount in. Tell your callee that you've no more change. Quote the number, so she can ring back when the time runs out.

You're in the habit of ringing a relative at the same time every week. She looks forward to your little chat. One week, forget to make the call. Tell her later, 'You know, my memory's starting to fail me lately. Perhaps it would be safer if you rang me from now on.'

When visiting friends, recollect, with a start, that you should have made a desperately important call. They'll show you the phone. In accordance with etiquette, your offer to pay will be swept aside. If it isn't, have no change.

If you can't get through to a number, never ask the operator to dial for you. You'll be charged for this. Ask her to check the number for a fault, then redial yourself.

You make a business call, and you're asked to hang on because the person you want is on another line. Tell the receptionist you're a doctor and need to talk to him very urgently indeed. If the person you called then accuses you of hurrying him under false pretences, ask politely if his boss knows he prefers to take personal calls while customers have to wait.

Telephones can be used to send messages absolutely free, even over long distances. Simply work out a code using the bell. For instance, if you want to let someone know you've arrived home safe after visiting them, you can arrange to give three rings on your return.

 Do the same to let people know you've set off. If you're only prepared to answer one person after a busy day, ask them to signal their identity by giving just two rings. They should then replace the receiver, and dial again.

## Cheaper Long-distance Calls

If you buy a phone with a special button, you can make long-distance and international calls through Mercury instead of BT. You'll save up to a fifth on mainland calls and a quarter of the price of an international one.

## Public Telephones

Phone cards are cheaper in the long run, because you get exactly what you pay for. If you use a 50p piece, you might only need 20p worth of conversation.

Feel about in the returned-money tray before dialling. A previous caller may have forgotten to reclaim any extra coins. They certainly don't belong to BT, and you can hardly go searching for the real owner. If you're near a row of kiosks, at a rail station, say, grope around all the trays.

## Professional Fees

Can we always trust all dentists and opticians? There's no doubt that some dentists are tempted to make money by filling healthy teeth, and that the odd optician presses customers to shell out for spectacles they don't really need.

Ask your dentist if the drilling she proposes is really necessary. Request the charges before the treatment starts. And resist all entreaties to have the work done privately. There'll hardly be much difference in quality between the two services, when there's a professional reputation to keep up.

Choose an optician who still offers free eye-tests. He also has a legal obligation to give you the prescription afterwards, so you can take it round to one of those shops selling less-expensive frames. Don't bother to feel sorry for the bloke. He still does very well, thank you.

# Do-It-Yourself

Know when to spend and when to spare,
And you need not be busy; you'll never be bare.
— *Thomas Fuller*

MOST people who do their own painting, decorating and general handiwork waste money in the overrated pursuit of perfection. This cult of the perfect is encouraged by manufacturers keen to sell more tools and materials than you need.

It's also fostered by desperate writers of do-it-yourself manuals. They detail a host of useless extra steps in a bid to: (a) appear knowledgeable; and (b) fill their pages somehow.

True, you may get a better result if you heed all they say, but the effect is so marginal, no normally sighted visitor will ever notice your superhuman effort. After a few weeks, you won't either.

Consider, too, that no finely decorated house was ever described by an estate agent as 'a home of character'.

There now follows ways to cut corners you won't find in do-it-yourself books . . . but first ask yourself if you need to decorate at all. A newly painted lair suggests working-class pride, while your aristocratic householder is never adverse to a bit of genteel decay. Many country mansions have state rooms, only because they're in a state.

## Free Materials

Decorating materials are hellishly expensive in chain stores. Even more so in small do-it-yourself shops. Avoid them.

Begin by poking around your garage or shed. You'll find a forgotten treasure trove of half-empty containers of paint, turps, wallpaper stripper, varnish and paint remover. Some, no doubt, abandoned by previous incumbents.

Try mixing the paint to produce the shade no one else has thought of. Tins of white are very useful as a mixing base, to make the resulting colour go a lot further. For example, just a dash of light blue, added to a lot of white, produces nearly the same shade of blue.

Don't waste time trying to soften old, stiff brushes with white spirit. Plonk them in paint remover instead.

If your shed doesn't produce the goods, ask relatives if you can look through their decorating leftovers. Arrange to borrow their pasting tables, paint scrapers and step-ladders, too. Who needs hire shops when you have friends?

If you're friendless, buy your tools at those auctions where household effects are sold off. My trusty step-ladder cost 25p in a sale room.

Another wheeze is to beg any paint abandoned by decorators at the office. Or take an interest in skips outside shops undergoing renovation. Farmyard sales are worth a look as well.

And keep your eye on skips outside houses in the latter stage of conversion to flats. Contractors use large tins which are often discarded while still half full. You'll have to be satisfied with magnolia and white though (magical colours which make box rooms look like bedrooms).

## Free Building Materials

You get these by lurking around housing sites. On average, fifteen per cent of bricks, timber, tiles, slates and guttering is discarded by professionals impatient of minor imperfection. A smear of cement or a brick can put it on the reject pile. A plank, three inches short, will be burned.

Site foreman are glad to push these rejects onto anyone who wants them. A friend built a garage for nothing, with a book from the library and rejects from a housing estate. He took them away piecemeal in his car boot.

Skips are also a free fount of household bricks, floorboards, architraves, skirting board, plastic guttering and drain pipe.

*Legal point*: you can take anything without permission if you've good reason to believe the owner is throwing it away. Leaving it in a skip or near a dustbin seem like 'good' reasons to me.

## Not-quite-free DIY Materials

Car boot sales, and of course garage sales, are rich sources of leftover do-it-yourself goodies. Shake tins of paint and varnish to make sure they're mostly full and that contents aren't solid. Haggle like Billy-o over the price.

Junk shops, too, harbour gallons of unloved paint. Their tins may look scruffy, but contents are durable, and colours rarely fade. If the paint has skin and lumpy bits when you get it home, strain it through old tights. And stir more vigorously than usual to raise pigments from the bottom. Otherwise your walls will get darker as the job goes on.

Market stalls often specialize in decorating materials. Usually this

is bankrupt stock, a result of the high number of small DIY shops which fall victim to chain stores.

You can also get paint at silly prices at those emporia which have elaborate machines for mixing different shades. When the process backfires, the results are sold off very cheaply to get a quick sale, and avoid embarrassment all round. Don't worry. You'll see, from daubs of the new colour put on the side of the tin, that most of these original hues aren't that bad.

Army surplus stores often have cut-price paint for sale. It's good quality – and not all battleship grey.

Wood and bricks are best bought at builders' yards which concentrate on second-hand materials. There's a whacking price difference. The wood is well cured, and used bricks have an attractive mellow appearance.

Demolition contractors often sell off the perks of their trade, too. You can get some real bargains if they happen to be murdering a Victorian building. Stained glass and intricate plasterwork are not unusual booty.

## Colour Schemes

If you choose strong colours, you'll be fed up of living with them long before you tire of pastel shades. More money will go drainwards doing it all over again. Paler shades will make your home seem spacious. It will raise more if you decide to sell.

## Painting the Outside

You can stave off the evil day when your house needs repainting by discouraging your neighbours from starting on theirs. No one will realize the task's overdue until a new paint job next door shows up your home.

Say something flattering like, 'I don't know what make of paint you used on your house, Jane, but it's certainly good for a few more years yet.'

When the time comes, you won't need a blowlamp to burn down to the wood. Those extra layers of paint protect against the weather. You'll also have to spend money on both primer and undercoat. Instead, use a scraper to deal with the flaky bits.

There's no need to buy sandpaper and filler either. Who notices lumpy bits on the outside of a house, especially bedroom windows? When painting bare wood, don't apply an undercoat. It's expensive. Use cheaper white emulsion instead. Then slosh just one coat of gloss paint over the top.

Don't skimp on the quality of exterior paint, though. The best stuff could save you getting your ladders out again for years to come. And stay clear of dark paint outside. It absorbs the sun, blistering easily.

## Avoiding Indoor Painting

Does your interior woodwork really need repainting? A light going-over with sugar soap may be enough. Perhaps it just needs retouching here and there. Only minute examination will ever reveal this has taken place.

Instead of repainting your doors, it's just as cheap to loosen a few screws and send them to a stripping firm. Doors in natural wood give an opulent look. And they'll never need painting again.

And why paint (or paper) behind large pieces of furniture, like bureau bookcases or large cupboards, which you've no intention of moving. It takes about two weeks to forget completely whether you got your brush behind them or not.

## Successfully Skimping on Preparation

Commercial fillers are pricey. Use newspaper soaked in water for large holes, then skim with filler. Use toothpaste on smaller holes and hairline cracks. (We would all save a lot of money at the dentists if Polyfilla worked on teeth.)

## Painting

Try emulsion pastel colours on windows and skirting boards for a change. You'll be surprised how much cheaper (and more sophisticated) this is than the ubiquitous white gloss. However, gloss is better on radiators and doors, where it's easier to wipe clean.

If your newly painted walls have patches of the old colour showing through, don't give everything a second coat. Whatever the experts say, you need only paint over the affected areas.

Gloss paint will go further by adding clear gloss varnish by one part to three, or in a 50 per cent mixture if the paint is a dark colour. Don't use white spirit. You'll only need more paint.

Wear rubber gloves to save wasting turps on your hands afterwards.

## Wallpaper

Why do experts tell us to peel off old paper, fill any imperfections and then paste on lining paper? All before we add new wallpaper. Are they in league with manufacturers? Do they begrudge us our free time?

The best way is to leave the old paper where it is. It is, after all, an old friend. Use it as both crack-hider and lining paper.

In fact, the more layers of old paper on your walls the better. They keep heat in and the sound of noisy neighbours out. Time-honoured rolls of old paper are probably holding your even older plaster onto the walls anyway.

It's true that earlier wall coverings might start to peel away when you apply the new, but you can always paste that back, too.

Even if you decide to emulsion the walls, you can always paint the paper rather than plaster. This gives a nice textured look.

If you must strip the walls, this is probably the only decorating job – as it is a kind of demolition – which can be safely delegated to children. If you haven't got any, pay a nominal sum to the gawky schoolboy next door.

Dispense with bottles of wallpaper stripper. Just put lots of washing-up liquid in hot water. Buying, or even hiring, a steam stripper isn't financially worth the small saving in effort. And it uses electricity.

Having woodchip on the walls is like coming across a murdered body. On no account attempt to move it. It can take weeks to strip one room of painted woodchip. All you can do is repaint it.

## A Good Pasting

A good pasting table can be improvised by an ironing board with a length of hardboard balanced on top.

Wallpaper paste goes further if you add a few pints more water than is recommended on the packet. Ordinary flour and water is nearly as effective, with a dash of floral disinfectant, perhaps, to act as a fungicide.

Many wallpapers are cunningly designed to cause maximum wastage. This is done by leaving a foot or more before the printed pattern is repeated. You need to unfurl more paper before the various flowers and scrolls will match up.

The problem could be avoided if the makers located patterns in the middle of the roll, leaving the edges plain. But of course they don't. So fight shy of extravagant designs.

When buying paper always exact a promise from the store that any unwanted rolls can be returned.

Remember that every inch of paper used may make you break into a new roll. So if you make a mess of a difficult bit (you cut too much paper away around a light switch, say) don't peel the whole length away in disgust.

Prepare an artistic patch by cutting out some of the pattern from a piece of waste. Then stick it over the missing bit. This gives a 3D effect which looks more like an embellishment than a repair.

Shops are often stuck with three or four rolls of discontinued stock. As this won't cover a room, the price is slashed. But you can paper just two walls, and emulsion the others in a matching colour. This makes rooms look longer.

## Free Wallpaper

Try papering children's rooms in old comics. SuperTed, Dennis the Menace and Batman are all likely to be popular. If this effect could stop you kissing your children goodnight, leave one or two walls plain.

Teenagers might accept the idea of acquiring dozens of different wallpaper samples (from separate shops) and pasting them up as a collage. You'll need to make them think it was their idea.

## Ceilings

If a white ceiling gets flaky, wash it down with one ounce of alum (from the chemist) in two pints of water. It will whiten and seal without painting.

## Floors

Why do we spend a fortune on underlay and carpet to hide the natural wooden beauty of our floors? Is it because the do-it-yourself industry makes stripping and varnishing floorboards seem such hard work? Well, it isn't.

You don't need to hire one of those large sanders like a lawn mower, and a hand-held one for the corners. You don't, therefore, have to hammer down all the nails below the surface to protect these unwieldy machines. Even sandpaper isn't necessary.

Simply use a razor blade to chip off the odd paint splash. Then get a bucket of soapy water and scrub the deck clean. Wire wool will see off any stubborn grime.

True, the wood will still be stained. It won't shine like a brand new ballroom floor. It will, in fact, look its age, and be much more interesting for that.

Any ingrained grubbiness can be disguised by buying a stained, rather than clear varnish. Dilute this with 25 per cent white spirit to make it go further and give the floor a coat. (Applying varnish is much quicker than paint.)

Leave overnight, then give the floor one more covering with varnish. Despite what the tin says, the floor will not need three coats – or sanding between each application.

Another even cheaper way of showing off floorboards is to paint them. A matt brown makes the room look really antique. Or use brighter colours to match the curtains. Eventually painted boards get scuffed. But this effect, often featured in magazines on period living, only adds to the charm.

Bare boards are *not* cold to the touch. They make a room feel warm. You'll never have to buy carpet, underlay, carpet cleaner or stain remover. You'll have no need of a carpet-fitter.

Ironically, going without carpet makes a room appear expensive. Your polished floor will subconsciously remind visitors of Buckingham Palace.

## Getting Carpeted

Now that your floorboards are varnished, you can raid junk shops and salerooms for second-hand rugs and Victorian carpet squares. Dirty specimens are exceptionally cheap. Once you've cleaned them, you could find yourself owning a valuable antique. Ancient carpets from the East fetch big money.

I once bought a long roll of expensive stair carpet at auction for half the price of the bottle of shampoo to clean it. And the stair-rods were thrown in.

Have no truck with one of those vacuum machines which clean carpets. Like sandwich makers, you'll probably only use it once. You won't even need carpet cleaners or foams. They're too dear.

Just add warm water to the kind of detergent used for hand-washing woollen sweaters. You can bring out the colours with a mixture of water and vinegar. Use a cloth to smooth it on sparingly, and dab it off. The vinegar smell soon disappears, together with any pet smells that may have lingered on.

Really filthy rugs can be treated by dunking in the bath. Professional carpet cleaners will wring their hands at this, as pile may shrink and colours may run. True, but if you really have a good carpet on your hands they won't. So it's worth the risk. Bathing carpets also kills cat fleas!

Less grimy carpets can be livened up by sprinkling flour, porridge oats or salt on them. Leave this mess overnight, then vacuum it off. The muck is absorbed.

## Professional Carpet Cleaning for Nothing

Offer to look after the neighbours' dog or cat when they go on holiday. On the day before they return, leave the animal in the room with your dirtiest carpet. Lock the door for twenty-four hours. When the inevitable happens, the owners will offer to have the carpet cleaned.

## Pictures

Those brass hooks with two pins are wasteful. Neither is it necessary to plug a wall to hang a picture. Just take a hammer to a nail. The picture will hide the crudity of this method.

The cheapest way to stick a poster on the wall is to use toothpaste at each corner. It will wash off afterwards.

## Tool Care

Whenever your car has its oil changed, mix the old contents of your sump with sand in a bucket. Store your tools by plunging them into this mixture in the shed. This keeps them sharp and free of rust.

## Employing Professionals

Doing it yourself isn't always saving money. If you earn more than a decorator or carpenter, consider spending the time you would be floundering around at home, doing overtime at work instead. Then use part of that extra money to pay the expert.

After all, a full-timer won't spend all day papering round one light socket. He won't get electrocuted. He'll own his own tools, and get materials at trade rate.

If opportunities of doing overtime are limited, you may be able to pay in kind. Tradesmen all need accountants, lawyers, motor mechanics and gardeners. A teacher could offer extra maths lessons. A musician could give piano tuition.

Take on a one-man band, rather than a bunch of employees. Overheads are less and a sole operator takes more pride in the work.

Don't, whatever you do, employ a company with a brand new van. They only prospered by charging too much.

Very often tradespeople have the impressive initials of a trade association on their vans and letterheads. They may charge you more money to cover their fees to join these organizations. Hardly a magazine or newspaper article is written on home improvement where a reader isn't advised to make sure their worker is a member of the so-and-so organization. But the advice isn't always sound.

You may feel you're in safe hands, but most trade bodies don't even monitor the standard of work of their members. And if there's a dispute, they protect the firm more than the customer. Some very respectable professionals will have nothing to do with them.

A safer precaution is to insist on written quotes for the work, not estimates, from three different sources. At this stage it's worth asking if you can act as a labourer to keep the costs down. They'll instruct you as the job progresses.

While employing professionals in your home, you might be able to borrow some of their gear – like ladders and paste tables – in the evenings and at weekends. Try and put them back in exactly the same place. They can get touchy.

## The Bill

Just before the plumber or joiner finishes the job, bring him a surprise cup of tea. Then timidly ask 'What's the damage?' This gives you the psychological advantage. His bill is likely to be less, because he won't want to upset someone who has just been kind to him.

Never let a tradesman say he'll send you an invoice later. He'll only use the delay to consider how much extra he can make you pay. Insist on settling when he's tired after a day's work – and may forget to add certain items.

## Repair Men

If a domestic gadget, like a dishwasher or washing machine, breaks down, don't automatically pick up the phone. See if you, or a handy neighbour, can find the broken part and remove it. (Many modern appliances are simpler than you think.)

Then send it to the manufacturer and ask for a replacement. There's no need to send any money or stamps. Just enclose a hard luck story about how it's always going wrong. When the bit comes back, put it back on.

If you do have a repair man in, and he gives you a piece of

paper to sign afterwards – don't. You could be agreeing that you're satisfied with the repair – so if it's ineffective, you can't have it redone.

## Double-glazing

Apart, perhaps, from blotting out traffic noise, you don't need it. The money saved on heating costs will take years to offset the huge expense of having it done at all. Instead, put a sheet of cellophane over the inside of the window frame and tape it down. Then go over the area with a hair dryer to tighten the 'inner skin'.

After a few winters, you'll be so adept at this job, it will take only a few minutes. Much quicker, in fact, than the annual wrestling match of cleaning double-glazed windows.

## How to Get the Better of the Highways Department

Sometimes, some of the paving stones in your street will subside, or the gas board may dig up the road outside your home. An official then goes down the road marking, in yellow chalk, the areas which need repair. Naturally, he'll miss out blemishes which are on the border line.

If he ignores an unsightly patch outside your home, encourage your child or a neighbour's to play with some chalk on the pavement. She might accidentally ring the right spot in yellow.

## Professional Sharks

. . . or three ways in which builders will try to rip you off.

 While doing the one job you ordered, they'll suggest several others while still on the site. They might say, 'Look what happens to this when I kick it.' Or they'll try emotional blackmail: 'If you don't do anything about it, that chimney will fall and kill someone any day now.' These 'repair' jobs will, in reality, be unnecessary. Plead poverty.

They'll keep asking for money in advance, then disappear before the work is complete. Keep forgetting to go to the bank and pay for each stage in arrears.

Some of the bricks and timber on your site mysteriously disappear. The builder blames thieves. But the gear will have been transferred to another house he's working on. Inform the builder a neighbour saw the theft. Being a kindly sort, the neighbour is waiting a few days in case the stuff is returned, before giving a description to the police. Just watch how fast the theft is 'reversed'.

## Labour on the Cheap

Listen to local gossip. Has someone been made redundant? Is a newly retired neighbour bored? Peer through windows to check their handiwork standard. Offer them cheap rates at your home.

Tell the family there'll be no summer holiday this year. You have to spend the usual fortnight decorating instead. 'The only hope,' you say wistfully, 'is if someone helps me to do it before the due date.'

Advertise on your own works notice-board for any handy types who want to earn pin money in their spare time.

Ask friends if they have any unemployed offspring who may benefit from a bit of 'work experience'.

Ask your tribe to invite the local decorator's children round to play. An open tin of gloss paint left in the lounge could cause a messy accident. The mortified parent may want to repair the damage by repainting the room.

If you're a pensioner or disabled, you may get your home decorated for nothing under a youth opportunity scheme. Don't worry – these beginners are supervised by experts. Apply to the council.

 Remember that if any of your ceilings or walls need repainting because of burst pipes, accidents or storm damage, the insurance company should pay up.

Do not, however, bother with the played-out wheeze of inviting friends round for a 'decorating party'. If any one ever fell for that one, they certainly won't do now.

## Curtains for You

Good curtains are expensive, especially those made to order in shops. Yet velvet curtains, which cost the earth new, are only a few pounds in urban auction rooms. They're invariably sun-faded, so give them a turn in the washing machine with a fabric dye. Your curtains will now have an attractive crushed-velvet look.

Bathrooms can be transformed by dyeing curtains, bath mats and faded towels all in the same fashionable colour.

## Fitted Kitchens

Why do many people feel they have to spend thousands of pounds on so-called 'designer' kitchens, which, as often as not, turn out to be badly-glued mismatches of plastic and artificial wood?

Try this instead. Ask a joiner to build you a room-length plywood worktop with a hole for a drainer and sink. Stick tiles on the top. Put your washing machine, dishwasher and fridge underneath. Ask the plumber to connect the sink, taps and washer, and an electrician to wire it all up.

Put curtains on wires across the spaces still available to hide pots and pans, and ask the joiner to add a drawer for cutlery. Fit matching curtains at the windows.

Old plate-racks and wall cabinets can be bought cheaply in junk shops for the walls. An old pine table will add a rustic look.

Your new kitchen will be just as practical and certainly more stylish than those plastic designer kitchens – at a fraction of the cost.

## Free Home Security

As you get wealthier, you'll become a target for burglary. But many of the security systems on the market already amount to daylight robbery. Here, then, are some free ideas which won't needlessly annoy neighbours at 3 a.m.

Fake burglar alarms are as effective a deterrent as the real thing. Simply paint an old biscuit tin bright yellow. Print the word Acme or Securex on it in black. Then hammer it high up on the upper-storey brickwork with masonry nails.

This decoy will easily fool the amateurs who perpetrate most break-ins. And a well-trained member of the striped jumper brigade knows how to foil a real burglar alarm anyway.

Try taping strands of wire along the inside window ledges. Would-be raiders will assume your windows (and doors) are linked to a sophisticated alarm bell system.

Saving cash on window locks is easy. Screws can be put a few inches up the sides of sash windows to stop them opening too far. Casement windows can also be held by threading a single screw through a hole in the sliding catch and securing it to the frame.

And you don't need a dog to fit 'Beware of the Dog' notices on both front and back gates. Another good deterrent is to tape a magazine photograph of a pit bull terrier to your window. Potential thieves will think it belongs to you.

Only a real professional will gain entry if you do all this. But if he does, placing a copy of the *Police Gazette*, or *Karate Times*, in the hall should soon send him scurrying out the door.

Incidentally, if all these deterrents fail, and you do hear somebody prowling downstairs, don't tackle him. Instead run into the street shouting and banging two dustbin lids together. Don't, however, follow the unfortunate example of one of my neighbours who took this conspicuous course of action while forgetting to put any clothes on!

# Gardens

It is saving, not getting, that is the mother of riches.
—*Sir Walter Scott*

TENDING soil is back-breaking. For many people all that digging,
pruning, mowing and weeding is also downright tedious. Worse
still, plants and shrubs cost the earth, especially at money-grubbing
garden centres.

But you can't let your land go to seed. A well-kept, colourful
patch signals you've arrived. It shows you've enough wealth, time,
health and sympathy for the environment to give the world a good
show.

A scrubby patch of weed in front of your home marks you out –
not as someone who doesn't care for gardening – but as a feckless
ne'er-do-well.

You don't need to spend a lot of time on your patch, though. Put
a card in the newsagent's window for a retired person to help you
out. Or tack an ad to the notice-board of a tower block where elderly
residents, missing a garden, will flock to your door.

An experienced gardener knows lots of penny-pinching short cuts.
And it's not necessary to pay them anything. Just share all that fruit,
vegetables and flowers they produce.

## Bargain Tools

Garden implements haven't developed much over the centuries. So
there are plenty of good, strong, hand-me-down spades, forks, hoes,
and shears around. They're of better quality and balance than most
garden tools just off the assembly line.

It's more blue-blooded to be seen with battered tools, which could
have graced the family for generations, rather than garishly red and
green models straight from the shop.

Find your elderly garden gear at garage, jumble and farm sales, as
well as in job lots at auctions. Or in the new shed when you move
house.

## The Spade Ruse

Let the children see you put a large number of coins in a bowl. Then announce a new game. 'Shiver-me-timbers, I'm burying pieces-of-eight in the vegetable patch for ye, Jim, lad.'

Tell them they mustn't look. Plant only a tiny few of the coins, then give them the spade. It's a piece of cake to finish off the job once they've given up in disgust.

## The Garden Centre Racket

Just like weeds, garden centres are everywhere. It is, after all, a nice sort of place to own. Customers like visiting them for their colour, fragrance, and warmth on chilly afternoons. They're set out like mini leisure parks, for family outings. But don't be fooled. It's your money they're after.

Prices can be awesome for something which began as a humble seed or cutting, originally costing nothing. Unlike other purchases, there's no redress if your plant dies the minute it's brought home. You can't prove it was their fault.

Sometimes proprietors will try to sell you, at knock-down prices, sad specimens with frost damage. You'd be green to think you can revive them with loving care. A frost attack is nearly always terminal.

On the other hand, some plants, stunted or damaged for other reasons – like an attack of insects long since flown – can be genuine bargains. It's worth taking a chance.

Garden centres also sell outside 'accessories' like stone gnomes, plastic urns and bright green frogs. Ideal – for anyone wanting to advertise their complete lack of taste to the entire neighbourhood.

We're also invited to buy many newly invented labour-saving devices, like patent watering gadgets, which, if they were any good, would have been invented years ago.

So all in all, if you want to save cash, drive past garden centres with your head down.

## The Joy of Gardening

It's much more fun counting your money and hunting for bargains than battling with muck, manure, thorns and crawling nasties. But gardening is associated with the monied gentry, so you must be seen doing it. Assuming that you've very little practical experience, here's a quick guide to basic, but impressive, soil tilling on the very cheap.

## Free Flowers

Cram your beds with perennial herbaceous plants or flowers which seed themselves every year. Favourites, almost impossible to kill, which multiply like crazy, include the larger daisies, foxgloves, lilies, golden rod, poppies, lavender, pinks, lavatria and nasturtiums.

These varieties spread so fast that many of your neighbours will be anxious to dispose of some of them. Simply lean over the fence and admire them. The plants will be uprooted before your very eyes.

Dig a hole, plonk them in and slosh water on, preferably when the sun has gone down, to stop them drying out.

You can also beg cuttings. Cut a shoot from the main plant above a bud. Then strip off the lower leaves, and put the cutting in moist soil in a pot. No one plant is the same, though. So plunder the library for a book on propagation.

We all learn at school not to snaffle plants from the wild, but ivy is an exception. It's quite expensive to buy it in pots, but in my experience a piece taken from a crumbling wall on a country walk lasts much longer.

## And Now to the Beds

Bedding plants add oodles of colour, but only last the season. They include petunias and lobelia. Seedlings can be bought in trays from market stalls, but are easily raised from seed. Use old egg boxes or margarine tubs with holes punched in the bottom, instead of seed trays.

Egg cartons are best because you can cut them into compartments, then, at planting time, you can put each one in the ground with the seed still inside. The cardboard will disintegrate.

Keep seedlings well watered in moderate light. Once all danger of frost is past, and they're big enough to handle, plant them outside.

Or you can take a chance and sow straight into the ground in May. If you have the patience, cut the base from plastic soft drink bottles to protect your tiny plants from the cold and insects. Remove the screw top as it gets warmer.

Alternatively, window frames from nearby demolition sites can be propped up with bricks to make cold frames.

When your flowers die, don't forget to take seeds for next year. Dry them in the sun. Then keep them labelled in paper bags in a dark places. A desk drawer will do.

## Free Seeds

As you walk through parks or past front gardens, no one minds if you pocket a few dead flower heads. They're full of seeds. And taking them is hardly a criminal act, as 'dead-heading' does flowers good, helping to produce more blooms.

It's not quite so acceptable to acquire cuttings like this. But if you fancy an unusual specimen in someone's garden, they'll be very flattered if you knock on the front door and ask permission to snip a bit off.

## Bargain Bulbs

Crocuses, daffodils, and tulips are real friends to the money-conscious. They multiply every year with no help from us. Trouble is, they make such a colourful display that few gardeners like to part with them.

One exception is the bluebell, which spreads through gardens like wildfire. You'll have no trouble cadging some of these pretty flowers, which have the advantage of thriving in dark spots.

A very cheap way to collect all spring bulbs is to buy them in November when the planting season is just about over. This is when market traders and supermarkets try desperately to give them away. They may not flower in the following spring, but they'll keep on coming every year afterwards.

## A Bed of Roses

Good value these, with well-known advantages: they flower all summer, and bloom every year. Which makes up for their twin disadvantages: they need pruning every spring and love horse muck.

It's a very aristocratic pastime, cutting roses (just above the bud) and composing them in a basket over one's arm.

The leaves can be collected and put in pot-pouri bowls. This does away with the expense of chemical household deodorants. Rose petals can be scattered in the bath too.

## Save It With Flowers

It's profitably far-sighted to grow flowers ideal for cutting (daffodils, tulips, roses, irises, lilies, carnations, gladioli and chrysanthemums). Otherwise buying bouquets for weddings, funerals, sick relatives, depressed friends and times when you have to say sorry, is an expensive business.

Why not make up your own bouquet with a piece of cellophane, to deliver yourself (long flowers at the back, short ones to the fore). If anyone sends flowers to this household, or to anyone at work, I usually appropriate the florist's paper for future use.

It's rather tacky to produce flowers personally, at least on formal occasions. But you could leave the offering on the doorstep, ring the bell and run off. Or local urchins could be hired for delivery duty, via the bus.

One occasion when a hand-to-hand exchange of flowers is necessary is the visit to a sick friend. If the sufferer has a large front garden, it should be possible to pick a few blooms for that last-minute bouquet. This practice can't be condemned as stealing if the owner ends up with the booty anyway. It is, in fact, a kindness, as the bed-ridden probably can't enjoy their flowers any other way.

If the person you want to send flowers to lives in another town, shun the flower delivery network at your local florist. Instead ask Directory Enquiries to give you the number of a trader near the recipient. Ring him up, ask for a quote, dictate your card and send him a cheque. That way you'll avoid a hefty, hidden service charge.

A final point about flowers. Should any unkind soul begin to suspect you're on the stingy side, a surprise bunch of flowers from your own garden, presented for no apparent reason, will correct the impression. And it still won't cost you anything.

## Organic Gardening

Put it about that you're a green gardener. Then you can leave a large area of your garden to grow wild as a mini nature reserve. Going green also frees you from buying chemical fertilizers and insecticides.

Consider this. Your gravel path needs constant weeding. So you buy chemicals to kill the greenery. This stuff also despatches friendly insects which attack pests and feed birds. The cat may be at risk. Eventually the poison ends up in the water system.

And are chemicals really quicker than pulling weeds by hand?

After all, you have to go to the shop, queue at the counter, come back, mix the stuff, water it in, and return to the house for several refills.

Then you have to buy another watering can, because weedkiller will taint the old one. Chemical killers aren't cheap, neither is petrol, or a new can.

## Muck-spreading

Everyone loves an organic gardener. So there's no shame in being in the street with a bucket and spade. Many plants, especially roses, like used tea-leaves and banana skin dug in around the roots.

A good liquid fertilizer is made by soaking ten egg-shells in a gallon of rainwater for a month. Don't be alarmed by the uninviting pong.

Compost heaps are free, too. Pile up all your garden waste, including grass clippings and fallen leaves. Add kitchen waste, like cabbage leaves, bits of sprout, potato peelings, egg-shells and even newspapers.

If it doesn't seem to be breaking down, add salt from time to time and a bucket of water. The resulting brown stuff is dug in around vegetables and flowers. You'll never buy a bag of peat again.

## Pests

Eschew costly insecticides. Spray your plants with soapy water, instead. Washing-up water will do. It won't harm plants. In fact, fruit trees thrive on soapsuds.

Or persuade your younger children to collect carnivorous ladybirds to introduce socially to greenfly.

Save more money on slug pellets by scattering soot or ash around your produce. They don't like it. And when birds finish off the slugs, they won't be poisoned as well.

Cats can be repelled with dried lemon or orange peel. Grind it up into a powder, and sift it round your plants.

## The Grass War

Only a large lawn justifies the expense of a power mower. Owners of modest patches should keep fit by getting one of those old-fashioned cutters which you push. They clutter second-hand shops, and grace jumble sales. Dose with an oil can, and sharpen with a file.

If you have a large expanse of grass (and careful readers will have one soon) get a reconditioned petrol-driven model – at a third of the price. Or consider buying two sheep – they're cheap if past their sell-by date, or you can resell them.

I know someone who has done this. Not only is her green sward immaculate, but she makes money hiring out her gluttonous mutton to neighbours. And she sells their fleeces once a year.

Goats and donkeys aren't suitable, by the way. They eat everything else, too.

## Cheap Garden Paths

Paving stones are like golden eggs, costly and difficult to lay. But you can make a garden path with the same effect for a fraction of the cost. Here's how!

Position two planks or old floorboards 18 inches apart, like railway tracks. Prop them up with a layer of sand down the middle. Push smaller pieces of wood crossways into the sand at 2 ft intervals. Mix concrete and pour into the squares.

Take away the wood when set, or leave the cross-pieces in to discourage weeds in the cracks. You now have a beautifully faked paved path.

## The Importance of Urns

Period stone and metal urns in the garden put you in the top drawer. But Georgian and Victorian versions can set you back hundreds of pounds. Fortunately, you can now buy a marvellous aerosol spray, which Medusa-like, turns plastic urns into stone.

Flowers planted in old stone sinks, chimney pots and worn terracotta look right. Those lodged in wheelbarrows and plastic urns don't.

## Instant Ponds

Look out for an old tin bath. They have no antique value. Even planted flowers can't liven them up. So they often turn up in skips. Simply dig a hole in the garden and put your bath in it. Disguise the metal rim with flattish stones.

This 'pool' can be made to look larger by burying other containers, like old buckets or washing-up bowls, next to the big one. Disguise the joins and fill in the gaps with trailing plants, like aubrietia (easily grown from seed) or Rose of Sharon.

Children will be entertained for hours, at no cost, by adding sticklebacks or tadpoles. Or you could go mad and buy goldfish. But, because your pond is shallow, the water will need changing occasionally, to stop it going green and smelly. A few oxygenating plants, lifted from a nearby stream, will also help.

Now here's a funny thing. If you install such a pond in the front garden and erect a twee notice saying 'Ye Olde Wishing Well', romantically minded passers-by will toss coins in. Put a 50p piece in yourself to start the ball rolling. (Stick it down with glue, before adding the water, just in case.)

Like all the more audacious ideas in this book, this worked very well for me.

Instant ponds, from old bath tubs, also make enticing additions to the estate agent's sales pitch when he tries to sell your home.

## Barmy Barbecues

Don't buy these or have them built. They'll tempt you to go to the expense of entertaining other people. And anyway it's a labour-intensive way of spoiling lunch. There's also something suspiciously *nouveau riche* about brick barbecues.

## Bird-feeders

Sausage-shaped nylon nets, filled with peanuts, are big sellers. But it's cheaper to buy a metal container, and refill from nuts sold loose in pet shops.

An even more economical way to feed birds is to mix seeds from home-grown sunflowers with used fat, heated in a saucepan. Suspend a piece of string inside a cardboard yoghurt container and pour the molten mixture around it.

When set, peel away the cardboard, and hang from a tree near the kitchen window. Yet another free entertainment.

## On the Inside

Indoor greenery is living furniture. It's cheaper to buy a potted palm than an occasional table to fill that boring space in the dining room.

Aspidistra, spider plants, and Swiss cheeses are almost impossible to kill. Rubber plants and palms are a bit temperamental at first, but live long once they get going. For colourful durability, at minimal cost, choose begonias, and busy lizzies. But keep them watered.

Indoor plants won't cost a penny if you take cuttings from your existing plants or those of friends. (It's funny those explanatory cards, which tell you how to look after your plant, never mention how to reproduce them. I wonder why!)

Many specimens, like spider plants and mother of thousands will produce miniature plants without any help. Simply pull the 'babies' away from the main bit and replant. You can cut a cheese plant into bits and plant any piece with a root on. Others propagate differently, and it's best to consult a book.

Once you have the knack, though, you'll be able to give scores of birthday, Christmas and Mother's Day presents without parting with another penny. You can even take a plant to a party instead of a bottle.

Indoor plants which outgrow your home are in big demand by restaurants, hotels and town halls. You can get surprisingly high prices for them by advertising in the local paper.

## Caring for House Plants

The most common cause of death in house plants is lack of light and too much water. Many a dying wreck can be revived though, by sending it on summer holidays to the garden.

And waste no money putting an artificial shine on your leaves. Use milk instead.

A last word on house plants – one huge specimen adds style to a home. A collection of twenty small ones has the opposite effect.

# Transport

*A shilling spent idly by a fool, may be picked up by a wiser person.*
*—Benjamin Franklin*

ASK yourself, 'Do I really need a car?'
Isn't it cheaper to use mini cabs, taxis, buses and trains? Might be, you say, but using public transport is fiddly. It takes time.

But does it really take much more of your life than queuing for tax discs, waiting for AA men, adding oil, water and antifreeze, refuelling, arranging insurance, hoofing back from garages, jump-starting, changing tyres, finding parking spots, sitting in traffic jams, and so on?

There are many hidden advantages of being without a car. You'll be fitter, wealthier, less stressed and anxious. You may even arrive earlier than a motorist because (some) trains are faster and taxi drivers don't (usually) get lost. You'll be regarded as a Friend of the Earth.

It won't even damage your affluent image to be without a car. Like Royalty, you should arrive for special occasions in a big black vehicle driven by an employee. It's called a taxi. And it gives the impression of extravagant wealth. (To cut costs, it's best to hail taxis in the street about half a mile from the venue. Travel the first bit by bus.)

## Ten More Reasons to Shed Your Car

 No more heart-stopping moments involving big lorries.

All that money from the sale.

No more embarrassing moments pushing it down the street.

No more covering the windscreen with newspaper, even on mild spring days, because you forgot to buy a tax disc.

You won't be expected to visit relatives quite so often.

You can drink as much as you like.

Pedestrians spot more bargains in shop windows.

You can rent out your garage.

You can always hire a car for special occasions – like a summer holiday.

 Uninvited visitors and rent collectors won't be able to tell that you're at home, by your car in the drive.

## Buying a Car

If you must have a car, don't buy it straight from the assembly line. You see as many new cars hooked to breakdown vehicles as old ones.

My Morris Minor is one of the most reliable cars ever built. On the few occasions it needs attention, repairs are cheap. A mechanic can get a spanner to *all* the engine. And he doesn't need to be a computer expert.

Motor engineers take more trouble with older cars because they like them. They enjoy working on Ford Populars and Triumph Heralds so much they forget to overcharge you.

Older models don't depreciate either. And you can find them again in car parks.

Cars depreciate most in their first two years. Buy one at the end of this period, and you get a better bargain.

If none of this discourages you from buying a brand new car, remember to ask for a discount of at least ten per cent for cash. You might need a bank loan to do this. But that's cheaper than any HP terms a dealer could arrange.

Beware of dealers who try to charge you VAT on the total price of a used car. They can only make this full charge on new vehicles. VAT is only levied on the profit margin of a second-hand car. Unscrupulous dealers, and not the taxman, will pocket this difference.

## Car Auctions

Cars sold under the hammer fetch much less than the book price. This is because most are fleet cars entered by large firms, electricity boards, the Post Office, the Armed Services and police forces. It's often thought they've been hammered.

In reality, fleet cars are well-maintained and regularly serviced. And they're hardly likely to have been driven by teenage road-hogs or dim-sighted grannies.

## Buying Tips at Auctions

Always go the week before you buy to get the 'feel' of the place. This allows time to get over your initial shock at the bargain prices. You'll be able to make a more considered judgement next time.

Trial spins aren't allowed, but you will be able to inspect bodywork before you bid. Make sure the car is firm all over. Take a magnet to check for filler. Engines are repairable. Rotting metalwork is another matter.

Never bid against private individuals, especially married couples. Carry on bidding only if your opponent is a dealer. They drop out long before the auctioneer reaches the market price.

Dealer-spotting is easy. They dress down to hide the fact that they make a lot of money. They look crestfallen, not excited. Their bidding is hardly discernible.

Remember to take a can of petrol to an auction. Sellers, just as mean as you are, will have siphoned off most of the petrol.

## More Ways of Buying a Used Car

Don't go to a garage. They buy cars or, more usually, part exchange them with private motorists. Then they add 25 per cent on for sale to the public. You can avoid this premium by buying directly from the seller.

Find out if a friend or workmate is set on the latest model, then make a keen offer for her existing car. Explain that she'll get a big discount for her newly acquired cash at the showroom.

Or keep your eye on the small ads. A private owner, unlike a trader, isn't obliged to take a faulty car back, if you're not satisfied. But, if you insist on a full MOT and check for rust, you should be safe.

Private sellers are vulnerable to haggling. Many owners form an attachment to their car, so don't criticize it. Simply make a low offer. Then evoke the greed factor by flashing notes. A wad of fivers looks more impressive than £20 notes.

You could also say, 'It's not easy when you've lost your job and must have a vehicle to work as a mini-cab driver and visit the little boy in hospital.' The owner will wrongly assume you're talking about yourself, and accept your offer.

If all this fails, walk towards the door . . . and up the path if necessary. If the bluff doesn't work, you can always come back.

## Avoiding Unreasonable Repairs

Many motorists only patronize large well-known garages. They believe them to be more reliable than back-street repairers. This is a mistake. Big firms employ more sixteen-year-old beginners than small ones. They pay more rates, rent, and advertising bills. Guess who pays for all this?

Proprietors of small garages will fit cheap second-hand parts. And you can actually talk to the man who does the job.

If this man is an employee, discreetly ask for his telephone number. Though this may lead to a misunderstanding, he may be prepared to do all your future repairs in his spare time for pin money.

But whether the garage is big or small, you'll be ripe for over-charging for unnecessary repairs if it's thought you are mechanically illiterate. So learn something by heart from the manual about torques and manifolds. Quote it to the proprietor. You don't have to know what you are talking about.

I always take my car to the garage wearing dark glasses, especially in winter. This gives a sinister appearance which garage proprietors don't like tangling with. They daren't overcharge a potential gangster.

Never lose your temper with an incompetent garage hand. Revenge is taken on the bill. If the tab is bigger than the written quote you were wise enough to get, threaten the garage with a traditional enemy – the Trading Standards Officer. TSOs hate garage men for keeping them too busy.

Personally, I never have my car serviced until it stops going. I'm told this is false economy, so I'd suggest that you change a six-month service to nine months. That way you'll only stump up four times in three years and not half a dozen in the same period.

If you cut down on servicing, it's prudent to stock a pair of jump leads. These are very satisfying, because it means getting someone else's energy for nothing to start your car.

If you have an older car now out of production – a VW Beetle or Triumph Herald, say – don't take it to a specialist garage. They're too used to dealing with enthusiasts bent on perfection whatever the cost.

## The MOT Rip-off

MOT testing can be expensive for the unwary. There's too great a temptation for work-hungry garages to find non-existent problems. Insist on being present during the inspection. Ask for any faults to be demonstrated. Examine discarded parts.

Innocently mention that if there are too many repairs, the car will have to be scrapped.

But it's not a sound idea to distract the tester by shouting, 'There's a wasp behind you,' just as he's about to discover the worn steering pin. Saving money like this won't help you if you bash into a tree on the way home.

## Feel Like a Spare Part?

Go to a wreckers for second-hand parts. Many will be on the shelves, but others will still be stuck like rocks to the parent car. Don't strain yourself with a spanner. Ask one of the staff to detach your part. Ring up first to save wasted journeys.

Dismantlers won't guarantee parts, but money is returnable if they don't work. Back-street garages don't mind fitting parts you bring in. It saves them driving off to get new ones.

Don't turn your nose up at remoulds. Even brand new tyres aren't always reliable. But second-hand tyres should be treated with suspicion. What happened to the car they were on?

Sometimes, though, a nearly new car goes to the wreckers after an accident. It's obvious the spare tyre would be worth the risk of buying.

## Saving on Motoring Bills

Washing your car with a sponge and bucket takes no more time than driving to a filling station and queuing for their pricey automatic machines. And you'll save on the occasional cost of a new aerial, too.

Remember that when antifreeze makers recommend 'correct' amounts, they err on the side of too much (wouldn't you?) Lean in the opposite direction.

The way to get distilled water for the battery is to save water when you defrost the fridge. If your battery expires, most garages have used ones to sell. Some of them need as many batteries as they can get to start the kind of cars they sell. Ask for a bigger battery than you had before.

Never join the AA or the RAC until you need them. Wait until you break down, then call and say you'll join on the spot. Or ring both, and promise your business goes to the first organization to get there.

Don't bother having a radio cassette player fitted. Buy a second-hand cassette player and put it on an empty seat. Do without battery-operated car cleaners, air fresheners and other useless motoring gimmicks. Use a dustpan and brush, and keep the upholstery clean.

## Ten Things You Didn't Know About Saving Petrol

 You may only get 10 mpg for short journeys as the engine warms up. Quick trips also cause heavy pollution. Walk to the corner shop.

A car with its choke out only does 7 mpg.

Find two filling stations opposite each other. They'll be fighting a price war.

Reverse into your garage at night. This saves making difficult, fuel-consuming manoeuvres to drive out in the morning when the engine's cold.

Keep sparking plugs clean.

Park in the shade to stop petrol evaporating.

Offer someone a lift. Pull up for petrol. Then remember you left your wallet at home.

You'll have a lighter touch on the accelerator pedal if you drive in slippers.

Stay away from the car in front and you'll drive more smoothly.

Driving in rain reduces fuel efficiency by 10 per cent.

## Bargain Motor Insurance

If your second-hand car isn't worth much, don't lash out on a comprehensive policy. Insurance companies are so mean, you will probably end up paying more for full cover than they'd give you back if your car was written off. And even if the other car you smashed to smithereens was a Rolls-Royce, a cheap third-party policy will pay for all the damage.

## Cheaper than Cars

If your nerves can stand it, swap your car for a more economical motorcycle. After all, they're favoured as much by the upper class as the lower one.

And a cycle, or better still a tandem, is socially acceptable. But, sad to say, no one ever cut a stylish dash on a scooter or a moped. And, of course, tricycles will never be fashionable.

## How to Park

Deliberately leaving your car in a restricted area is irresponsible, but just in case you do it accidentally – if yellow lines have been obliterated, say – you could leave a *Police Gazette* on the shelf below the rear window. Those rubber gadgets for washing hair which look like stethoscopes may also give the impression that you're a doctor on call.

But we can't sympathize with those miscreants who park in schoolyards or on council property by putting *Teaching World* or *Municipal News* on display.

People who put 'No Parking' signs outside their homes have little justification. But if you need to park there, leave the car with its bonnet up, giving the appearance of a breakdown. Or disconnect a sparking plug, and leave a truthful note on the windscreen: 'Sorry. It won't start.'

If someone in your family has a disability, apply for a parking sticker from the Council.

## Selling Your Car

It is no social disgrace to dispense with a car these days. Just a sign you care for the environment. But whether you're selling your vehicle for good, or want to buy a better one, don't dispose of it to the tight-fisted trade. Use local newspapers, especially those which advertise free.

Or let your car be its own advertisement. Stick hand-written 'For Sale' signs in the front and rear windows. It may take longer, but it works.

As with estate agents selling a house, there's a glossary of terms for potential buyers:

*Good little runner* – It won't pass its test.

*Smart condition* – The engine has had it.

*Rust-free* – You are not charging extra for it.

*30,000 miles recorded mileage* – The other 100,000 miles is not recorded because they went off the clock.

*One careful owner* – Six others weren't at all careful.

*Collector's car* – Suitable for a black museum.

A good time 'psychologically' to sell your car is just before the milometer hits one of the 10,000 figures, never just afterwards. Then tell potential customers the only available time to view is during the evening (when it's too dark to see properly). Warm up the engine just before they arrive.

Take them for a spin, but explain that you must do the driving 'because of insurance problems'. Then distract them from the vehicle's performance by chatting about the advantages of that particular make generally. Say 'Fords start easily' or 'Maestros use very little petrol.' No need to mention that yours is the odd one out.

If they can't make up their mind, say, 'It's up to you of course, but I've had at least ten other phone calls.' These were from your boyfriend over the last three months. But you never said they were about the car, did you?

Insist on cash, otherwise your cheque might be stopped when your customers realize their mistake. Remember you do not have to return money as long as you didn't tell the buyer any fibs.

All these tips are offered as expedients for selling a car which is roadworthy. If anything about your vehicle is dangerous you must, of course, confess it.

And now that you are without a car you'll need to learn . . .

## How to Use Cars Without Actually Owning One

Going to a social event, like a wedding, dinner dance, darts match or a party? Ask a fellow guest to pick you up at home, as you're not sure how to get there.

Persuade workmates that you could all save petrol by taking turns to drive everyone to the office each day. After a while, you could remove a battery lead from your own car. Then continue to get a daily lift, truthfully saying, 'Sorry, but my car won't start in the mornings.'

Organize a school run, in which you and your neighbours take turns in ferrying the kids to school. Then drop it into conversation that your car is a bit of a death trap. You will soon be left out of the rota, though your children will still be catered for.

On a day when it's essential you turn up for work, ring up the boss to say your ankle has 'gone funny'. You can't walk or drive. In desperation, a taxi will be ordered for you.

If you have a long journey planned when others are likely to be making the same trip, going home for Christmas, say, or bank holidays, advertise for a place in their car, on the works notice-board. Or insert a small ad.

This is an even better idea for people who work in large cities during the week and would like a lift home every weekend.

## Dealing with the Taxi Man

Taxi drivers come early. They know you'll have to pay for their waiting time. So order your cab five minutes later than you want it. And be ready on time. Better still hail your taxi in the street.

If you already know the fare for your journey, from home to the station, say, ask the driver if he'll take two pounds less. Otherwise you can only afford the bus.

People standing in line for taxis, outside a station perhaps, should canvass the queue for others going the same way. They should then pretend to be friends and all share the fare. If cabs are scarce, this kind of deal also saves time. It makes queue-jumping respectable.

If you choose a cheaper mini-cab firm, ask for a price before you set off. Then mini-cab drivers, who haven't got meters, won't be tempted to inflate the fare on arrival, when it's too late to argue.

The first thing to let your driver know, by indirect conversation, is that you were born locally. This will stop him favouring the longer route.

Then ask, 'How's business?' When you're told, inevitably, that it's poor, you reply, 'Well at least it's better than being made redundant on a day when you're expecting your fourth child.'

He will rashly assume you're talking about yourself and, as taxi drivers are only gruff on the outside, no tip will be expected.

When sharing a taxi, you obviously need to make somebody else pay. The cross-over technique is best here. Sit in the rear near-side seat. On arrival ask the cab driver to pull up on the opposite side of the road.

Then, with a show of good manners, lean across to open the door for the person sitting next to you. He will then find himself outside in a natural position to pay the driver, who may well stick his hand under his nose.

Afterwards make a lame attempt to reimburse the payer, perhaps when he's busy struggling with a suitcase. Such offers are normally refused.

Cab drivers, busy in the evenings, do a lot of unprofitable hanging around in the day. So if you can interest a party of five in a long trip, like a day's Christmas shopping in London, then you could have a chauffeur-driven service for less than six return tickets on a train.

Don't disclose how much money you're paying the driver, and you might even get yourself a free trip. This, of course, is why teachers arrange ski trips for sixth-formers.

## The Train Game

Use season tickets, City Savers and rail cards where possible. Watch out for free ticket offers on soap packets and chocolate bars. Avoid travelling on Fridays and bank holidays when it can be more expensive.

First-class tickets aren't worth bothering with. The seats aren't much better. You'll also be bored silly with loud shop talk from expense account sales people.

British Rail put a free glossy magazine only in first-class coaches. There are no rules to stop you collecting one on your way to a second-class coach. The cleaner first-class toilets are available to all, too.

In some trains, first-class style seats are labelled 'second class' near the buffet. You only need buy a cup of tea to sit there.

If all the second-class seats are full, complain to the guard that you are not your usual self. (Who ever is?) Ask if you can sit down in the first-class section to recover. He won't have the heart to evict you if you're still there two hours later.

Save time and the cost of a hotel room by using sleeper accommodation. Or better still travel on a milk train with one of those blow-up cushions round your neck.

Take a vacuum flask, your own lager tins and sandwiches on a train. Mashed banana or egg are cheapest. All this saves swaying about queuing for an expensive but limited choice if, that is, the buffet happens to be open.

Buffet staff are notoriously short of change. Board with a bag full of silver and negotiate for a free cup of coffee and a bun. Sounds daft, but it has worked for me.

Never buy your own newspaper or magazines to read on trains. Borrow from fellow travellers.

There's no need to pay extra to reserve a seat. Most people who do this are also cautious enough to arrive early anyway. They then take the first available seat to avoid searching the train.

All you have to do is take the reserved seat for yourself, when the train sets off. In the unlikely event of the reserver arriving later, you can always move . . . into another vacant reservation.

Should you prefer the luxury of empty seats around you, place a piece of electrical flex with bare wires protruding between the seats. Would you want to sit there?

If your train is more than 30 minutes late – or less if you miss your connection – or it's cancelled altogether, write and ask for a refund. At first, they'll refuse, referring you to BR's conditions of travel. These say they don't actually guarantee to get you there.

This could be laughed out of court as an 'unreasonable clause' in a contract (the one you struck when you bought your ticket). However as far as I know the point has never been tested because BR are prone to settle out of court if pressed. So keep trying. And claim a bit more than the ticket price as compensation for the inconvenience.

You can pay to insure your luggage, but if you leave it in the guard's van you won't need to. British Rail will pay for thefts or breakages, but won't if you leave it in the luggage racks.

## Coaches

These can cost a third of the cheapest train fares. They take longer, but only if your destination isn't on a motorway. Coaches don't break down as often as trains do, and the bus station may be nearer your home than a rail station.

Modern coaches are comfortable, and sprung well enough to make reading easy. Refreshments are brought to your seat, and I find the staff cheery. Fortunately, the eccentric video movies they used to show have now been taken off by public demand.

Should the coach pass near to your home, you should ask the driver to stop before he reaches the terminal. Even if he's not supposed to, he knows nobody will report him for being kind.

Tickets have to be bought in advance. It's easiest to use high-street travel agents. Discounts are available for off-peak travel. But, of course, for the adventurous, the only real way to travel is by hitching a lift.

## Ten Sneaky Ways to Hitch A Lift

 Stand by an empty oil can. Drivers who think you've run out of petrol will stop, thinking, 'There but for the Grace of God go I.' Leave the can behind as though it's nothing to do with you. If your benefactor mentions it, deny all knowledge.

Drivers would rather pick up one person than a group. If you are travelling with others, one should thumb while the others lurk behind a bush. As most drivers who help hitchers are men, it's best that a woman should do the thumbing.

Carry a cardboard sign saying where you want to go. But if you're travelling quite a distance, write down a destination which is only a part of the way. Break the news to the driver later on.

Wear a camouflage jacket. You could be mistaken for a member of the armed forces. Drivers called up for national service will recall the rigours of getting home for leave and will be glad to stop.

When a car passes you sink down to the grass verge with your head in your hands. Any driver, looking in the mirror, may take pity on you.

Look as young as possible in your dress. Some motorists feel the only people entitled to hitch are students on a tight budget.

Stand towards the end of a straight stretch of road, not a bend, to give drivers good time to make up their minds.

Dress casually smart. No one wants to pick up a smelly tramp. On the other hand hitch-hikers in suits tend to remind drivers of gangsters or confidence tricksters on the run. Try wearing yellow, a friendly, non-aggressive, reassuring sort of colour.

Walk along the road, your thumb working, while affecting a limp. Or hobble with a stick.

Drivers who stop at filling stations find it hard to refuse hitchers who approach to ask for a lift. Takes a bit of nerve, but it saves a lot of time. (Bear in mind that there's a lot of respect for people with old-fashioned cheek.)

## A Car That Doesn't Need Petrol

Though it's against my mercenary principles, I'm giving away free to all readers the idea for a car which has no running costs whatsoever.

It's a light one-seater with a battery-powered electro-magnet attached to the steering wheel. When a vehicle passes the end of your drive, switch on the magnet and point it at its rear bumper. Your car will be carried along behind the other vehicle.

When the other driver takes a direction you don't want, merely switch off the magnet. Reactivate it when a car comes along which is travelling the right way.

Mechanics, who are probably jealous, tell me this brilliant idea won't work. But I can't see why not.

# Lovely Money

If we take a farthing from a thousand pounds, it will be a thousand pounds no longer.

*—Oliver Goldsmith*

NOW that you're spending a fraction of what you used to, you'll have oodles of cash to spare. As everyone knows, money makes more money. But it won't grow under the bed. You must invest.

I won't undertake a comprehensive exploration of all the various hedges against inflation. It's a vast specialist subject. But as no frugalist wants to take any big risks, here are just a few tips on some of the safer courses of action.

## Building Societies

The safest places to multiply your money, especially when mortgage rates are high. The smaller give a better return. And as no building society has ever gone bust, they're as secure as larger ones. But they don't have as many branches, so only pick a smaller society if it has a branch near your home or workplace.

Pay money into building societies by cheque. Interest is credited from the day you pay in. But because it takes time to transfer that money from your bank, it's earning interest there too.

Your pay cheques will earn more interest if you save time by asking your employer to pay them directly into your building society account.

## How to Manipulate Banks

If your bank account goes into the red, don't roll over and accept the punishing bank charges and interest demands which follow. Write the manager a note: 'I'm sorry this happened. But the electricity and gas bills both came together this week, and the children find it so cold. Could you please waive all penalties on this occasion.'

After drying his eyes, he'll agree, to avoid feeling mean – and to stop your business going elsewhere.

The next time you overdraw the account, you may have to appeal to his sense of humour rather than his sympathy. Try this: 'As I've never pulled a face at any of the cashiers, will you forget about the bank charges if I stay in the black from now on?'

When writing to bank managers always use their first name. It's harder to refuse someone who seems to regard you as an old friend.

Be nice to bank staff. Never throw a wobbly if you're forced to wait in a long queue. Your unreasonable behaviour will get back to the manager. Yet you're bound to need a favour from him one day.

Should your bank accidentally bounce a cheque, when you're in funds, invoice them for £100 for the embarrassment caused. If the manager refuses, say you will 'ask for a second opinion' by mentioning the mistake to head office. Your compensation will arrive by next post.

Have nothing to do with a joint account. There's not much incentive to save money if your spouse is at large with another cheque book.

## Impressing Bank Managers

Bank managers are indoctrinated to believe that money is all that matters. This might be sensible, but it means you can't rely on their sympathy and kindness when pursuing a business loan or mortgage. All you can do is show that you're both parsimonious and wealthy.

Visits to a bank manager call for a white shirt or blouse and a grey suit. Psychiatrists say grey denotes restraint and respectability.

Show your confidence in your financial situation by laughing a lot and cracking jokes.

Managers are trained to notice expensive trappings. So sign any forms with a very expensive fountain pen, perhaps borrowed for the occasion. If your wrist-watch is tacky, go without one to the interview.

When writing to a bank manager, use good stationery. Go to the poshest hotel in town. Ask the reception for a batch of their headed writing paper and monogrammed envelopes provided for guests.

They'll oblige, as it's only printed in the cause of advertising. The bank will assume you have plenty of money if you can afford to stay at this hotel. This gambit is equally useful for canvassing orders and applying for jobs.

## The Insurance Game

Protect your home, possessions and health by all means – and your life if you've dependants you care about. But that's about all you should have to do with insurance companies.

Whenever someone tries to sell you any kind of life policy including endowments, resist like Horatio on the bridge. Succumb and you'll find that a large slice of your premiums go on 'administration'. And you'll get very little back if you ever need your money in a hurry.

What looks like a small fortune promised in twenty years' time will be a modest sum by the time inflation has taken its toll. In the meantime, the insurers have been enjoying your money at its proper value.

One weapon insurance salesmen use is the 'pitying look of horror' technique. If they feel you're about to reject their overtures, they gaze at you as though you've just thrown your future to the Devil. Don't fall for it. Put your money in the building society.

Use a high-street broker to arrange home, contents and motor insurance. They'll use computers to shop around for the cheapest quotes for you.

All companies who insure property try to make you pay premiums to cover much more than your home's market value. They claim that if you're burned down, the extra cost of demolishing and carting away the bits bumps up the cost of disaster.

They forget to mention that the market price includes the value of your land which can't be destroyed. This site value would more than make up for any demolition charges. In fact, the total cost of knocking down your old house and building a new one could well be less than the 'market value'.

Unfortunately, many building societies protect their commission from insurance companies by insisting you insure your home for more than it's worth. The way to counter this conspiracy is to get a quote from a builder on how much it would really cost to demolish and build a similar house. Then insist to the society that you insure only for that amount. They'll be left without an argument.

There's sadly no defence against another insurance company racket. It seems reasonable to under-insure the contents of your home, on the grounds that no burglar will manage to take the lot. But when the company discovers you've only covered half the value of your possessions, they'll only pay for half of your stolen goods, even if their value is just a few hundred pounds.

Soon – by following advice in this book – you'll be able to afford large diamond rings and oil paintings. Your insurers will want separate valuations. Don't pay a firm of professional valuers to call. Take your glittering prizes to a posh shop, offer to sell them, and ask for written estimates.

If you have a claim, many insurance companies begin by turning it down. This pays them, as many weaker souls immediately give up. Write back politely with a list of reasons why they should act honourably. If this fails, threaten court action. They hate publicity.

If insurers take more than three months to settle a claim, ask for the interest at building society levels, not bank rates. Complain to the insurance ombudsman, if you don't get it.


## Personal Pensions

Pension brokers, or 'independent financial advisers' as they optimistically like to be known, earn big rake-offs from insurance companies and banks – sometimes equal to the first six monthly payments.

Agree with your broker that you'll only take the pension if he splits his commission with you. Otherwise you'll deal directly with the company. He'll still strike a lucrative deal.


## The Time To Pack It In

Retire just after April 5, otherwise you may pay tax on any 'golden handshake' which could be considered part of your income.

## Getting a Loan

If you follow advice in this book, you'll never need one. But if you do, arrange an overdraft with your bank. Second mortgages, loan firms and 'easy credit terms' come a poor second.

A really painless way to get cheap money is to ask your insurance company to make you a loan on the security of your endowment policy. You'll only repay the interest – the capital can be taken from the lump sum when the policy matures.

Beware the expression 'secured loan'. Though it sounds safer than an unsecured loan, it means your home is forfeit if you can't repay.

Anyone who lends money will try to make you insure against defaulting on payments (to protect them, not you). There are cases where these insurance payments amount to half as much as the loan! Whatever the banks and loan companies do to make you believe otherwise – and they try pretty hard – you don't have to pay the premiums. And you shouldn't if you think your job is secure and your health is sound.

## Manipulating Mortgages

If your home loan is adjusted annually, you'll lose out if interest rates are cut just afterwards. Don't resign yourself to wait another year before your monthly repayments drop. Most building society managers will alter your interest rate almost immediately if you trouble to ask them.

Never completely pay off your mortgage. Owe the society or bank just £1. Then they'll continue to safeguard your deeds for nothing. They'll also be obliged to sort out insurance cover and claims.

## Credit Cards

Only the strong of will should apply. The exception is when credit card companies offer free watches, calculators, fountain pens and so on just to get you interested. You should accept the gifts, then throw the cards away.

## Ten Ways to Exploit Credit Cards

If you are strong willed enough to warrant a credit card at all:

 Always use your card instead of cash which could be earning interest for a bit longer in a building society.

Pay the debt off in full on the due date to avoid paying any interest.

Consult the monthly statement for the date it was printed. Then use the card most on the day or two before it's next due to be printed. The shop's paperwork won't reach the credit card company in time to be added to the current statement. So you'll get two months' free credit, instead of one.

When a shop accepts a credit card, it has to pay five per cent of the sale to the card company. Ask if they'll give you the same discount if you pay in cash.

Most credit card companies charge the same rate of interest. But a few, mainly merchant banks, charge less. Seek them out.

Don't use credit cards to get cash from hole-in-the-wall machines. Conventional bank withdrawals are cheaper.

Credit cards should be well used abroad. It can take a long time for your purchases to show up on your statement here.

If you accidentally build up credit on your card, by getting a refund from a shop, say, don't let it sit there. It won't earn interest. Ask the company for a cheque.

If you use your card to pay in advance for something, and the shop goes bust before you get it, ask the credit company for your money back. They're just as responsible.

 If you find a credit or bank card in the street, ask the bank for a reward. You'll get one.

## Lending Money to Someone

Never do it. Ever.

## Inheriting Money

The only honest way of realizing a lot of money you don't deserve is by being mentioned in a will. Increase your chances. Make regular visits to elderly relatives. Fill the time by commiserating about the other (perhaps closer) relatives who never bother to call. Discuss how profligate they've become. And innocently mention your own unjust money problems from time to time.

At first blush, this may seem like a dirty trick, but the elderly relative really benefits from your attentions. And they'll have no earthly use for their estate later on.

The same approach works for people working for elderly employers. Reading the papers, it seems housekeepers, handymen and chauffeurs do as well out of wills as they do in fiction.

## Unit Trusts

Buying these is generally safe, because your money is invested in the shares of many companies. But there are high administrative charges. Usually 5 per cent is deducted from the value of your trusts to begin with. Then there's commission to pay, of up to 1½ per cent per year.

Performance can be abysmal. Financial experts employed by unit trust companies frequently do worse than many amateurs in picking shares. And when you decide to cash in, you'll find that the selling price for unit trusts is less than the buying price. Personally, I think buying unit trusts is a mug's game.

## Other Investments

Many ordinarily sensible people have lost a lot of money investing in various financial deals, which promise returns well above average. Remember that if any offer seems too good to be true, it probably is.

## Income Tax

I bet you're paying more income tax than you ought to. Have your returns professionally checked – an accountant's fees are deductible.

It's heartening to know that she'll be able to look into, and claim for, any overpayments you might have made going back seven years. I once wrote to my tax man saying 'I think I might have been overcharged for quite some time.' Though I had no paperwork to support this, they investigated – and sent me a large cheque.

## Shares

These are usually safe, though not always, if you buy into well-established firms or utilities, like steel and gas. Safer, anyway, than Australian gold mines. All the statistics show, however, that the best returns are made if you leave your money in the stock market for some time.

It's now very easy to buy shares. Some building societies will buy and sell for you if you're a member (and that could be having just £1 in an account). Banks give the same service, whether you have an account or not.

Or pick a high-street broker, who, after the first transaction, will take your instructions over the phone. It's wise to choose carefully, as commission rates vary.

Always instruct your stockbroker loudly when the office is full. This benefits your image. It's also very satisfying to see the value of your shares rise when you scan the morning papers. For some reason it's not comparably discouraging to see them fall. You naturally assume they'll recover. And they usually do.

The best time to buy shares is when a nine-day wonder in the news sends all shares plummeting. As there are no changes in the company itself, the price is likely to bounce back. You'll then make money at the expense of panic sellers.

You can also strike gold by buying into a company which has envious eyes cast on it. A merger battle sends prices rocketing. Of course, you'd need to be very lucky to predict a takeover. But you may be able to act before other investors, if you read financial pages religiously.

But buying and selling isn't the only way to make money at shares. It's easy to forget there are useful dividends as well.

It's less hazardous to spread the risk by buying a small number of shares in a lot of companies. But this isn't really a good idea, as a minimum commission is payable when you both buy and sell. You would do better to invest more (at least £1000) in less companies.

Because of the commission taken by dealers, it's daft to sell one set of shares just to buy into another company, unless there's a very good reason. This is known as over-trading.

Before you do anything in the city, glean as much free advice from your stockbroker as you can. You *have* to accept that shares are risky (but doesn't it sound successful to have a 'stockbroker'?)

One way to do well out of shares, with no risk at all, is to buy a few hundred shares in a company which sells things you might need. An electrical manufacturer for instance.

Then sell all the shares except one or two. You'll still be entitled to any shareholder discounts. So your next TV or hi-fi set will cost much less. This works for travel companies and hotel chains, too.

## Paying Bills

Despite the fuss electricity, gas, water and telephone companies make, there's nothing wrong in waiting for the reminder before we pay their bills. This is one of the few ways we have of getting our own back for the high fees they charge.

More unscrupulous bill-avoiders will 'forget' to sign cheques. On return they'll write new ones, this time 'accidentally' undated. This can go on indefinitely. If someone uses this trick on you, send round a large male friend to collect a complete cheque in person. He should wear dark glasses, clip-on earrings, tattoo transfers and talk gently in an *EastEnders* accent.

## Gambling

If you share my tendency to hang on to money at all costs, you'll suffer more pain than most when you lose some of it to the fickleness of Lady Luck.

You can't make money at roulette, otherwise casinos wouldn't exist. You won't win on horses, otherwise bookmakers wouldn't be rolling in it. Indeed, some firms have done so well out of the betting public they've become international conglomerates.

Winning the pools might be as unlikely as being struck by lightning, but it could turn you into a millionaire, so it's worth a try. The cheapest way is to enter twenty weeks in advance with a standing forecast. It saves a lot of time, stamps and postal orders.

Entering competitions can pay dividends because, for once, the odds are on our side. Few people bother to enter puzzles set by food and soap firms; they're only arranged for advertising promotions. So your chances of winning are favourable.

In fact, some people make their living entering commercial contests. They may have to bulk buy to get the required number of labels to enter, but then there's always something to be said for buying and hoarding before the prices go up.

## Ten Ways to Win Competitions

Check for the right answers in the local library.

Send in as many entries as you can. Unless the rules forbid it, use the same envelope to save postage.

If answers are required on a postcard, cut out your own, making it bigger than the standard size. A large card is less likely to slip to the bottom of any pile, and is more of a draw to competition organizers.

Make your entry conspicuous. Cut it into the shape of an animal or the advertised product. Alternatively, cover it in glitter powder.

Use several ball pens in different coloured inks.

Make it simple for the judges by printing your entry in block letters.

Always include a phone number, even if it belongs to a friend. People who organize competitions love to advise people personally that they've won a prize.

If a tie-breaking slogan is called for, make it as original and as flattering as possible. Or adapt a slogan from a less well-known advert of a few years ago.

Entrants who are photogenic should overcome their natural modesty and enclose a photo. The publicity department may be looking for an attractive winner to appear in the press.

Using childish writing may win sympathetic consideration.

## *How Not to Win a Competition*

Don't be tempted to stick a pin in your entry. Anyone delving around in the pile may well pull out your effort with a screech. But they'll be too angry to add it to the winner's pile.

A dab of treacle on your entry won't adhere to a judge's finger, only glue your postcard to someone else's.

# Your Wardrobe

He that will not stoop for a pin will never be worth a pound.
*—Sir William Coventry*

## The Importance of Best-quality Clothes

Expensively dressed folk make a statement: 'As we are doing well in life we deserve your respect.' The message goes unheard by most of us. But it is picked up by other snappy dressers – members of the same club.

People in this secret society give and get favours. They bestow executive jobs. And they invite each other to top social functions.

If you buy clothes in chain stores you won't be in on the deal. In fact, you'll find it hard to spot who is well dressed and who isn't. Only by wearing top-drawer clothing yourself will you recognize a superior cloth and expert hand-stitched cut on others.

And once in this club, you're on your way. Members of the WDC (Well-Dressed Club) will always crash through class and accent barriers to the top.

Well-cut, pricey clothes say that if you're not an executive you ought to be. The rich and influential will employ you, buy from you, mix with you and rejoice if you marry into the family.

## How to Join the Club

If you're not already in the WDC it's because you recoil at paying £300 for a suit, £250 for an evening gown, or £300 for a posh mac. You can't see why huge sums are squandered for a label. Even if it is a Hardy Amies, Gucci or Giorgio Armani.

But you can join this classy fraternity without spending much. Buy exactly the same clothes with the same famous names. But not in Bond Street or Savile Row. Instead, go to charity shops, run by Oxfam, the RSPCA or Help the Aged.

This is how I own ten top suits all of 'timeless' cut. There's a Hardy Amies, an Armani, two Pierre Cardins, and an Yves St Laurent among them. I didn't part with thousands of pounds. Just £130 for the lot. Everything from the same charity shop over six months.

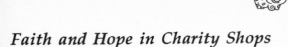 

## Faith and Hope in Charity Shops

The charity shop boom shows no sign of slowing down. My own small country town has four. Oxfam, the 'market leader', now has 830 branches.

But because most customers are down-at-heel, there's a myth that kind-hearted people who supply the stock are in the same impecunious boat. Yet the racks of MIND and Christian Aid bend with well-spun wares of the very best calibre. Here's why:

> Heavy-quality clothes outlast their welcome. Owners eventually get rid of them simply for a change.

> Those who dress well can afford to eat well. Growing tums cause constant wardrobe revision.

> Only the affluent can afford to pass on clothes before they wear out.

> The better-off have a long tradition of supporting charities. As they're fond of money, giving clothing salves consciences without much pain.

## The Right Stuff

Only charity shops in the very best residential areas will do. It's worth travelling to your nearest large city to seek them out.

Don't go to second-hand clothes shops which are run privately. Their profit-conscious proprietors know about market values. Charity shop assistants, on the other hand, are well-meaning amateurs who charge the same for good quality – and rubbish.

Shops which sell 'period' clothes should also be shunned. You may well find forties hats, sixties dresses, and teddy boy jackets at Oxfam. Buy them. Then sell them on to a period clothes shop (your conscience might want you to return some of this profit to the charity.)

## What to Buy

*Suits.* Let the labels be your guide. Legally, garments must give details of their materials. Choose natural stuff like wool, cotton or linen.

Make sure you know the good designer brand names. Keep a list if your memory's poor. Watch out for the Royal Warrant. What's good enough for Buckingham Palace is fine for you.

Never let anyone see the designer label on your purchase. Only the *nouveau riche* would stoop to this. Don't worry: people with breeding will know the quality of your garb instinctively.

Ironically, it's a good sign if a suit doesn't have a maker's label at all. It was probably hand-stitched by a small tailor, with good cloth

and pride in his work. There's a tradition among really good tailors to print the label upside down.

In men's suits, a buttonhole and obvious stitching of the lapels are signs of craftmanship.

One drawback of buying second-hand clothes is finding a perfect fit. Don't worry. If you can't shorten legs and sleeves, no doubt someone in the family can. More difficult gussets and seats can all be cut down for a few pounds at dry-cleaning shops. So can flared trousers.

If the outfit you fancy is too small, look for extra material along the seams which can be let out.

*Jackets.* Same advice as above. But it's worth remembering that charity shops often charge the same for a jacket as a two-piece.

*Trousers, skirts and slacks.* Beware of shiny behinds. But holey pockets are easily stitched. No one will see any ragged results.

*Jumpers and sweaters.* These are too prone to stretching to buy second-hand. Fortunately, for climatic reasons, jumpers are heavily reduced in January and July sales.

You could also learn to knit. Or cultivate a nimble-fingered relative. And home-made jumpers of individual design are sold cheaply by fanatical fireside knitters at car boot sales.

*Shirts and blouses.* Second-hand ones might not appeal. But if they do, look out for quality names and natural fibres, like silk or cotton.

*Underwear and socks* should be given a miss (as second-hand purchases I mean). But then there's no need to lash out anyway. Unless you are amorously adventurous, or accident prone, who's to see them? Buy in outdoor markets. There's also no shame in darning socks. You'll be conserving a vanishing art.

*Ties and scarves.* Silk sells at the same price as junk materials in charity shops, so look round for the best. But reject silk items with stains: they're hard to get out.

Watch out for ties with crests. There's no law against wearing a distinguished tie from a school you didn't go to. Eton, for instance, or Harrow. Or a famous regiment or club. I have a stylish, motifed tie rescued from a pile of jumble for 5p. Though it proclaims a link with the Sub Aqua Association, I can't swim a stroke.

*Footwear.* Being indestructible, really good shoes and boots are frequently retired to charity shops. Men's shoes should be heavy. Good women's footwear should feel soft and finely stitched. Names like Church's and Gucci will help. Check society magazines (the next time you are at the dentist) for the better makes.

*Belts.* Always plentiful, so you can afford to pick the best leather and finest stitching. Saddle soap and metal polish restores the most ill-used specimens to near-new condition.

*Hats.* Charity shelves are brim-full with them. From peaked caps to Edwardian creations with wax fruit and stuffed ducks on the top. It's funny how all headgear stays in fashion.

*Overcoats and macs.* Happily, these seem to breed in charity shops. Burberries and Crombies, very costly when new, are offered at the same giveaway prices as run-of-the-mill outerwear.

Fashion isn't a problem. Traditional long overcoats have been cut in much the same styles for most of the century, and good ones are everlasting. My own double-breasted black woollen overcoat belonged to a former chief constable of Denbighshire. That was thirty-seven years ago. It's still admired daily.

## How to Exploit Jumble Sales

Visit jumble sales only in the best residential areas and the rewards can be huge. Given the adversarial nature of this kind of bargain hunting, you need to be there first. The best way of doing this is to volunteer as a seller.

Otherwise you need to be the first customer into the hall. This isn't easy without enduring the indignity of waiting for an hour, in full view, at the head of something that always looks like the queue for a soup kitchen.

It's despicable to come well before the sale and switch the 'queue here' sign to the wrong door. But you could try paying one of the many children who seem to lurk around jumble sales, to stand in the line and save your place. To avoid infuriating other customers, one should say something like 'you can go home, Johnny, as your dinner's ready now' to give the impression the child is your own.

## More Tips on Buying Second-hand

You don't need a bag over your head in a charity shop – or at a jumble sale. After all, you are serving two good causes at the same time. The charity itself and conservation in general.

Ask if the garment has been dry-cleaned. Shops don't usually bother, but they may know if the donor did, before delivering to the shop.

## New Clothes

As usual, looking forward is the key. All new clothes should be bought in the January and July sales only. Target the very best shops. They make much bigger reductions.

Go on the first day, but don't queue all night. . . . I once began a 3 a.m. wait for a new suit, only to be at both the head and the tail of the queue when the store opened six hours later.

Beware of closing-down sales which don't display a final date. Some shops won't shut until three years later.

Seek out any unobtrusive imperfections. Draw them to the manager's attention. When a reduction is suggested, splutter loudly in protest. Embarrassed that the other customers will become aware that shoddy goods are on display, a much better offer will follow at the speed of sound.

Many modern shoes are designed to look fashionable, not to keep water out. But it they do leak, even if you only discover it six months after you bought them, you'd still be in the right to complain. Legally, all goods must be fit for the purpose for which they are sold. In the case of shoes, to keep your feet dry. The shop must give you a new pair or your money back.

In privately owned boutiques it's worth asking, 'As I may be buying quite a lot here, what kind of discount can I expect for cash?'

If you have a small build, try children's departments for clothes and shoes. They're free of VAT.

## Despicable Tricks to Make You Buy

Something like seven billion pounds is spent in British clothes shops each year. Much of this damage is caused by crafty sales staff on commission. You should be aware of some of the ploys they use to part you from your cash.

Inexpensive clothes seductively lit in artistic window displays are mixed on the same racks with much more expensive items inside.

Men buying a bargain suit are often shown a matching, but expensive, shirt and tie; women are offered a pricey matching blouse.

Some changing-room mirrors are designed to make you look slimmer. You think it's the effect of whatever you are trying on.

Watch out for clothes piled into rummage bins. This stuff is as dear as anything else in the store.

If you've spent a long time making up your mind, it's probably because the shop has nothing suitable. So ignore the pained looks of assistants who're trained to look hopelessly sad – and walk out.

## Excuses Not to Buy

If you are the breadwinner, there will, sadly, be many occasions when members of the family coerce you into shopping sprees to buy clothes which aren't for you. Inevitably, only the dearest garments will be picked out. To change their minds, without your real motive of saving cash becoming apparent, you should:

Say: 'It's absolutely stunning on you. I expect that style will soon come back.'/ 'Your mother will love it.'/ 'It's rather like the one Gaynor bought last year.'

Severely admonish the sales assistant for pinching the jacket at the back (even if she isn't).

Say you have sudden tummy trouble, and run from the shop.

## Other Ways to Build a Class Wardrobe

Seek out clothing manufacturers with shops attached to their factories. A growing trend, this. Prices are low because the middleman is cut out. Factory shops aren't always advertised by the way. Many firms are sensitive about antagonizing their trade customers.

Watch your local paper for bankruptcy sales in hotel rooms and auction houses.

It's worth calling in at wholesale fashion houses selling exclusive designs to the trade. Some of them, especially if they're having hard times, will bend the rules to sell to members of the public.

Market stalls sell good-quality casual clothing, particularly jeans and T-shirts left over from business failures. But beware of tatty track-suits and scrappy shirts from rag-trade unknowns.

It is often a comfort to the family of someone who dies to know that his or her clothes will be put to good use. So it's not bad manners to ask, tactfully, if you could be of help here. Similar, though more cheerful, enquiries can be made of friends leaving for Australia.

## Restoration

Shines on seats can be removed by sponging with a mixture of vinegar and water.

A bright dye can cheaply revitalize almost anything, giving instant colour co-ordination. Many people fear the results will be patchy. This won't happen if you use a washing machine.

Replace broken handbag straps with cheap gold chain from the ironmonger.

## Money-saving Accessories

*Handbags, purses* and *wallets* are rife at jumble sales, church bazaars and boot sales. Scuffed leather is much more stylish than new – and no animals will be newly slain to supply you.

*Umbrellas.* Don't buy an expensive one. They all look the same when furled and you'll mislay it sooner or later. Take advantage of someone else's bad luck at railway lost property sales. Newspapers announce them.

*Watches.* Famous makes can be snapped up for peanuts at local auctions. You won't strike such good bargains at second-hand jewellers or pawn shops, but you can get acceptable watches – as well as wallets, calculators, small radios and pens – as inducements to apply for credit cards and unit trusts. Simply pocket the free gift and discard the paperwork.

*Wellington boots* are more comfortable, watertight and cheaper than walking shoes. They never need reheeling, waxing, polishing or new laces.

## Useless Accessories

Never waste money on cheque-book holders, containers for £1 coins, passport covers, cigar cutters and the like. Pontificate to all around you how useless these items are to avoid getting them as Christmas presents.

## Making Clothes Last

Now that you're buying good-quality stylish clothes, they'll last much longer. You'll be able to go many months, years, without spending any more money. Here's how to make clothes even more durable:

Follow Margaret Thatcher's practice of packing tissue paper into pockets and shoulders to keep the shape of clothes hanging in wardrobes.

Change immediately after work into older clothes.

Rotate your clothes daily. Try not to wear the same outfit twice in one week. The fibres need time to recover.

Hammer metal protectors into your shoes.

## Ten Ways to Cut Cleaning Bills

Don't waste money buying and running an electric dryer. Clothes hung on the line smell fresher. They also last longer. Spin and tumble dryers cause wear.

Many items which look as though they should be dry-cleaned can in fact be washed. Check labels to avoid unnecessary bills.

Don't use a dry-cleaning firm just to remove a stain. Try a solvent instead. A suede jacket can be cleaned by hanging it in the steamy bathroom when you have a bath. Let it dry, then use a suede brush.

Patronize a small family dry-cleaners. They come cheaper than national companies.

Take everything to the dry-cleaners at the same time, and ask for a discount for bulk.

Don't take suits to the cleaners just because the creases have gone. Get the iron out.

If you need special clothing for your occupation, or if your work is grimy, cleaning bills can be put against tax.

Try using a dry-cleaning machine at your launderette.

Use half the amount of washing powder recommended by the makers. We all know what they're up to.

Think twice about buying anything in white.

Take the washing home to mother.

## Formal Wear

Now that you're in the expensive clothes club, fellow members will invite you to more dinner dances, concerts, theatre performances and charity occasions. You'll need formal evening wear.

Never buy evening gowns or dinner jackets in the high street. Don't go to hire shops either – too expensive. Instead . . .

Borrow from friends and workmates. Even casual acquaintances will be glad to oblige. It's something to do with boasting that they, too, have a social whirl.

If you borrow an evening gown you particularly like, say to the lender afterwards: 'It's very popular. At least three other women at the dance were wearing the same outfit.' Two weeks later you can offer to buy it – for a derisory amount, of course.

You're expected to have borrowed evening wear cleaned before you return it. Yet it has only been worn for a few hours. Save this expense by ironing the gear, after sponging off any wine stains. Then pop it into a polythene bag saved from your last visit to the cleaners.

## Buying Formal Evening Wear

Save a packet by buying only at charity shops. Nowadays individuality is as important as up-to-the-minute fashion for evening gowns. And styles from the sixties and seventies are considered chic. For men both double- and single-breasted styles are now acceptable, so the choice of second-hand dinner jackets is huge.

Flares can be cut down and cummerbunds can be worn to hide extra inches in the waist.

Buy your second-hand evening wear in the spring and summer. The choice narrows as Christmas nears.

## Evening accessories

*Cuff Links.* Gold-plating is as effective as the real thing on formal occasions. Fellow guests won't be bad-mannered enough to search around for hallmarks. But even 24-carat cuffs are cheap enough at suburban auctions. They often go under the hammer after a death in someone's family. Usually at half the scrap price.

*Earrings, brooches and bracelets.* Victorian, Edwardian and art nouveau pieces go for next to nothing in salerooms, once again when Great Aunt Matilda's effects are being sold off. Gold jewellery set with precious stones fetches surprisingly little. This is because old pieces often lack sparkle under a layer of grime. Soap and water works wonders.

*Pearls.* The cultured variety sell very cheaply second-hand. Yet it's hard to tell them from the real thing.

*Evening bags.* These often turn up at jumble sales. Misguided donors think they're unfashionable. But period bags are particularly admired by those in the know. And it's comforting that the dimmed lighting of dinner dances makes it hard to tell brass from gold, and diamante from diamonds.

## How to Pretend to Good Breeding

It's not only how expensive or well cut your clothes are which marks you out as a person of quality, but how you wear them. Here are a few pointers:

Never be seen without stockings or tights.

Carnations should be worn with the stem pulled tightly through the button hole, so that the flower is tight against the lapel. A floppy carnation with asparagus fern and other foliage attached is bad form.

Never wear a wrist watch with evening dress.

A gentleman rolls his sleeves flat against his forearm. They should not be squeezed into a tight wad just below the shoulder.

Track-suits and trainers should only be seen on running tracks.

Sorry, but in a green world, fur coats are out.

Sweaters must not have monograms on them.

Sports jackets should have leather patches on the elbows.

Socks should be the same colour as the darkest part of the shoe.

If you are caught wearing down-market clothing – a T-shirt with a slogan on it, perhaps – you can still pretend to good breeding by saying something in an upper-class way. Remember the aristocracy always understate everything. They would never remark 'I just don't *believe* this!' and an unusual incident is 'amusing', not 'fantastic'. A 'perfectly agreeable chap' is a top person's idea of a 'wally'.

## *To Sum Up . . .*

Everything you buy new becomes second-hand at the same instant. So why be too proud to buy handed-down clothes in the first place. If you seek out the very best quality, of traditionally fashionable rather than trendy cut, you'll look smart for a fraction of the cost of buying unremarkable outfits in the high street.

As well as having the money you saved in the bank, you'll have the confidence of knowing you dress well – so signalling your worth to everyone in the same well-dressed club.

# Grooming

A penny sav'd 's a penny got.
—*William Somerville*

YOU can only be a person of quality and substance if you're well groomed in public. (Don't, of course, bother about being smart in private.) Never fear: attention to personal detail isn't costly if you learn the ropes.

## Hair Today

As usual, the most expensive hairdressers aren't always the best. The tariff is just as likely to be influenced by the address and flashy interior design, as the expertise of the cutters.

Hairdressers improve with age. Greater experience helps them to achieve what you want. Any idea that they're out of step with modern styles insults their professionalism. They may secretly disapprove of your choice, but they won't be let down. Simply show a magazine picture of the style you want.

That said, styles of traditional cut are best for both men and women who want to attain high social position, and make lots of dough.

Shop around, and when you've found a talented hairdresser at a cheap shop, ask for that person every time. Then you can be overheard in the office making an appointment with 'Rosemary' or 'Justin'. This impresses the boss.

Many hairdressing parlours, and all hair-styling colleges, won't charge if they can let a trainee loose on your head. This isn't dangerous. Close supervision is given by old hands. The more prestigious the shop, the more onerous the training, and the bigger the bargain for you.

And remember that students will be so terrified of making a hash of it, they'll really concentrate. The one and only snag is that apprentices can take a long time.

Whether you're dealing with a trainee or an expert, you should never chat to a hairdresser. When they get overheated about politics, pop music, religion, or football, bang goes your coiffure.

It's wise to call in the morning, when stylists are fresh. By the afternoon fatigue sets in.

Flattery is a very useful tool at the hairdressers. 'Please cut it in your usual immaculate way. No one does it as perfectly as you.' This endows your stylist with an instant reputation she'll try to live up to. And fulsome praise after the cut is useful as a tip substitute.

The number of visits to a hairdresser per year can be halved by ordering it cut short and then letting it grow long, before calling again. But apart from shortening a fringe, or shaving a neck, never be tempted to economize by hacking your own hair. Don't ask mum to do it either. It always ends in tears.

## The Hair Care Caper

Like most cosmetics, there's little to choose between the ingredients in an expensive shampoo and those in a cheap family one. Glossy advertising causes the difference in price. That, and fancy over-packaging. Buy a cheap shampoo and impress fellow bathroom users by keeping it in an expensive bottle.

Better still, make your own shampoo to put in your posh container.

Add 2 teaspoons of soft soap and 10 drops of olive oil to three cups of warm water. Shake before use.

Most people over-shampoo their hair. Use half as much as you usually do from now on. You can also have a time-saving, dry shampoo, using less hot water. Leave baby powder or starch in your hair for two minutes. Then brush it out.

Conditioner doesn't seem to make a lot of difference to hair, given the cost. Natural yoghurt is just as good.

Dandruff isn't the loathsome disease shampoo-makers would have us believe, but if you must treat it, pour boiling water on nettle leaves. Leave to cool, then strain. Rub the liquid into the scalp.

## Nails

The first thing they tell students at schools of door-to-door salesman-ship is, 'No one notices clean fingernails, but they always notice nails which are dirty.' Keep them scrubbed. Nail clippers leave a better shape than scissors.

Professional manicurists do make improvements. But they're hardly noticeable, so save your money. You can always impress friends by saying 'I'm going to see my manicurist' when you go shopping.

## Eyes

Eye drops are pricey and messy in use. If your eyes have been taking a battering, have a nice cup of tea. Then put the tea-bags in the fridge for ten minutes. Place them on your eyelids, and lie down for a bit.

## Teeth

When your toothpaste tube is empty, stand it in hot water for a few minutes. It will last another week. When it finally runs out, try using salty water for a few days. It's almost as good. Breath can be freshened up by chewing a sprig of parsley from the garden.

## Soap and Deodorants

Liquid soap is wasteful. We pay extra for the dispenser, which is designed to make us use too much. Fancy perfumed soap is another dud buy. The working ingredients are standard. You pay for the package, the promotion and a transient smell.

Leave soap out of the packet for a week to harden. It will last twice as long. If you buy cheap soap without packaging it's even more durable.

Stick deodorants go much further than spray cans.

## Ten Ways to a Cheaper, More Luxurious Bath

Most of us are conditioned by advertisers into an obsession with personal hygiene. It's not necessary to bathe every day.

Why not follow someone from the family into the tub? This saves reheating water. And you won't be the one who gets scalded.

The price of bath salts makes it worth looking for substitutes. Mix ¼ oz of oil of lavender with 1 lb of salt and ¾ lb of borax.

Make a nylon bag by cutting the foot from a pair of tights. Fill it with raspberry or blackberry leaves. Dunk it in the water. Or hang it by a string under the hot tap as water runs through, squeezing occasionally to get more oil.

Almost any garden herb gives a relaxing soak. So (with care) do pine needles.

After swimming, have a shower at the pool's expense.

Adding salt to your bath will get rid of deep-down dirt and any oiliness.

Economize on hot water by making the bath seem hotter than it is. Add three tablespoons of mustard powder. Yes, it really works.

Staying overnight with friends is an economical time to take a bath.

Never stay in a hotel without having a bath 'on the house'.

## Hand Lotions

These never last long, so make your own. Glycerine from the chemist is the key. Mix it with lemon juice, witch-hazel, or honey. Add some rose water or lavender for extra luxury. Keep it in a screw-top jar in the fridge.

## A Close Shave

Shaving soap and foam isn't really necessary. Ordinary hot water will soften whiskers. And it trebles the life of blades. They won't get clogged. Blades can last and last by running them on the inside of a glass.

## The Sweet Smell of Success

Inform male friends that all but the very best perfumes give you a rash. A month later, muse aloud that you hope someone buys you perfume for your birthday or Christmas this year. Then wait.

If you can't trust anyone to buy you an expensive scent, decant a cheap eau-de-Cologne into an empty expensive perfume bottle. Give it a shake. The result will be both interesting and original.

Should the temptation to buy your own perfume prove too much, remember that even the poshest brands may not suit your particular chemistry. So shop in the morning when your sense of smell is keenest, and you're less likely to make a costly mistake.

## Make-up

Cultivate the natural look, and never be short of men friends. It's less tarty and costs nothing.

If you do use make-up, it can be removed with raw potato. Baby oil will shift eye-liner. So will sunflower oil, normally used for frying. Some swear that boot polish is more effective than mascara.

## Keeping Fit

Lots of contraptions are sold to keep figures trim. Most are expensive. All are unnecessary. Many end up on the second-hand market because they eventually bore their owners witless.

What's the point of buying an exercise cycle which goes nowhere, when you can have a real, second-hand bike to get around free? The amount of muscle toning is the same, and you'll get fresh air in your lungs.

Where's the sense in buying a rowing machine to strengthen your back when you get the same benefit digging the garden, growing potatoes and cutting food bills?

And why dig deep for dietary supplements, when you can reduce by eating less fattening foods? Will-power is free.

## Free Fun with the Sun

Expensive sun lotions have much the same ingredients as the cheap ones.

To treat sunburn, use a half and half mixture of vinegar and water. Soak a handkerchief and hold it to the burned skin. To maintain your tan, brew tea in a pot and pour it into your bath water. A couple of tea-bags perform the same trick.

## Inescapable Conclusion

The cosmetics industry is greedy for your money. Almost any of its products can be substituted with things from your garden or pantry. (And they won't have been tested on animals, either.) You can still look good by avoiding cosmetic counters altogether. How's that for a saving and a half!

# Holidays

He that will thrive in this world must think no course vile.
—*Ben Jonson*

STRANGELY, many people who are sensible about money for the rest of the year throw away all caution at holiday time. They make two wrong assumptions: that package deals are the cheapest way of living it up abroad for two weeks, and that the most expensive hotel is the best.

We buy package holidays because we think the tour operator can cocoon us from the devious ways of wily foreigners. But who protects us from the tour operator?

Doing without a package tour conforms with the guiding principle of this book – keeping out the middleman. And even better than rejecting the middleman is getting the better of him. This is done by holding your nerve.

Don't book well in advance. Wait till the week before you intend to leave, then study the last-minute bargains in travel agents' windows. They're offered when operators desperately try to sell holidays, cancelled by people with illness, bereavement, redundancy or a lovers' quarrel to contend with. The nearer the fly-by date, the cheaper they are.

You might not get the first country of your choice, but as foreign resorts all look alike nowadays, who cares?

If the nearly-unheard-of happens, and no such cheap holidays are available, book your own flight through a travel agent. Then search out somewhere to stay once you get there. This is not as difficult as the package industry, and their accomplices, foreign tourist departments, would like us to think it is.

These conspirators have an interest in supporting big hotels and expensive apartment blocks, but you'll get more of a feel for a place and pay half as much in a room in a local house.

Go to the harbour area (the most interesting part of town) and ask bartenders, who are always related to everybody, for likely addresses. Taxi drivers are similarly qualified.

Once settled in your ethnic abode, you can revel in the satisfaction that you're not paying package firm directors their percentage, as well as the wages and accommodation of an army of schoolgirl couriers who'd rather grace the world's sun spots than do a proper job in rainy Britain.

If your ethnic place of abode turns out not to be as wholesome as you'd like – or the resort reminds you of Hades – you can always move in a day or two. This is rarely possible if you're on a package holiday. And whatever your room's like, you'll be out of it most of the time.

Avoiding package holidays means you don't have to go to those ghastly 'welcome parties' where couriers give you indispensable advice like 'Don't go out in the sun' and 'Try not to poke about in dead trees, especially at night.'

The advice is duff, because that's not why the party was laid on. They really want to sell you corny, over-priced excursions which you can arrange a lot cheaper yourself (if you really want to).

The only reason many people choose package holidays is for the security of a coach laid on from the airport to the hotel. Yet, the most primitive airports have a regular coach service to town. You can easily check this, and the price of local taxis, before you commit yourself.

The second and third reasons for making your own arrangements are that it gives you self-satisfaction and a greater sense of adventure. The first reason is that you and your family really will save a great deal of money.

And you really won't get life imprisonment for vagrancy, or be sold into white slavery. I promise.

## Cheaper Package Holidays

If I still haven't managed to persuade you, and you really would be happier with a conventional package holiday, begin by getting hold of every brochure you can. The horror of meeting somebody in the same hotel who paid £300 less for a better room isn't easily forgotten.

The bigger tour operators can usually offer you a better deal because they 'buy rooms in bulk'.

Pay for your break with a credit card. If the tour operator goes bust before you leave, the card company has to make a refund. They'll sometimes arrange free holiday insurance, too.

If you cut out the agent by ordering your holiday directly from the tour operators at their address on the brochure, you can get a 10 per cent discount.

Most firms don't like to offend their middlemen by cutting them out, so it helps to say you don't live near a travel shop. You may actually live only twenty yards away, but distances mean different things to different people.

Some companies offer to take children either half-price or free. This kind of firm is best avoided by those without offspring. You'll be subsidizing them.

If you really like travel, work for a holiday firm. Employees get up to 60 per cent off some holidays and free tickets if seats haven't been sold on weekend charter flights. Counter staff are also asked to fly abroad to check the quality of service in hotels from time to time.

However much of a bargain package you get, you won't enjoy a cheap holiday if you choose a country where there's a high cost of living. Don't rely on friends for guidance. Rampant inflation may have taken its toll since they had that fabulous meal out in Greece for £2 with wine. Ask a travel agent, then get a second and third opinion from two others.

## Free Foreign Holidays

The cheapest foreign holidays of all are had by befriending someone whose family has a chalet in Spain, say, or southern France. If, despite all your hints, the offer isn't forthcoming, tell the owners you'll be passing near the site this summer. 'Would you like me to call in and check that everything's all right?'

People with property abroad always worry about theft, fire and flooding, so they'll gratefully hand over the keys. Naturally, a proper security inspection can take two weeks!

## Cheap Air Fares

All sorts of cheap fares are available if you fly in off-peak periods well in advance. Such forward planning isn't difficult when arranging annual holidays.

You can frequently save by flying first to a different country, Holland say, and taking another flight from there. Your travel agent will work it all out. Make sure your schedule is in writing. Then you can sue, inexpensively, in a small claims court, if anything goes wrong.

You can cut the cost of air travel by a half, or even two thirds, by acting as a courier. This is how it works.

There are agencies which help firms who need someone to escort private papers to foreign countries (across the Atlantic is a common run). These are legal documents or bank drafts which can't be entrusted to the post. The agency secures a cheap ticket for you, if you do the carrying.

Someone hands you a package and your ticket at the airport. Somebody else meets you at the other end. It's all pleasantly romantic, like being part of a spy network. But check you've not been encumbered with any white powder. Similar deals are sometimes worked out for escorting small children. You'll need to track these agencies down through Yellow Pages. They don't have to advertise such an obvious good deal in newspapers.

Sometimes we forget that aeroplanes aren't the only way to see the world. Boats and trains may take longer, but they're cheaper, and you see more.

Once, to save a few quid, I took a train journey from Leeds to watch the seagulls over Sorrento in Italy, while the rest of my party went by air.

A continental train strike got under way, and we were boarded by armed police in France. They escorted the driver through groups of angry pickets who regarded him as a blackleg. Angry scenes, involving pistol-waving, took place at every French and Swiss railway station, before we limped into Italy.

This Hitchcock-style adventure wouldn't have happened on a flight to Alicante. Not only did I enjoy the experience, but I demanded, and got, some of my money back for the 'inconvenience'.

## What to Take

Make a list of everything you'll need. Go through it and cross off at least half.

Don't follow tradition and buy a new set of holiday clothes. The rag trade pushes different swim styles every year, in the hope of selling more of something that never has a chance to wear out.

But there's not enough of a bikini to change very much. And they can't do much to shorts or T-shirts either.

No, take the same old holiday gear with you. None of those you meet in Costa Plenti will have seen you in it before.

If your holiday outfits or beach towels need smartening up, put them in the washing machine with a vivacious dye. This year's colour, of course.

It's worth putting coffee, tea-bags and Coffee-mate in your bags. Add one of those modest plug-in water heaters that looks like a kettle filament. This saves on notorious foreign cafe prices.

Paperbacks and films are cheaper at home, too.

## Tourist Information

There's no need to squander on foreign guide books or maps. All embassies and national tourist offices, based in this country, will send you their many publications free if you write in good time. Stamped addressed envelopes aren't necessary. They'll pay their own postage to get greedy hands on your sterling.

You can also get similar information for British resorts from county councils. And Trust House Forte do very good maps of Britain. Just write to them.

## Flying Tonight?

Don't rely on airport catering. It's clean, fresh — and hellishly expensive. Like their car parks, there's no competition to contend with. Bring your own sandwiches and fruit.

They won't stop you eating your own food anywhere in the terminal, except perhaps the cafeteria. Even then, the usual airport custom of ignoring passengers altogether should let you get away with it.

Don't buy magazines and newspapers. Politely borrow from fellow passengers.

## The Duty-free Scandal

The excise duty and VAT on a bottle of spirits amounts to nearly two-thirds of the cost. So you'd expect duty-free shops to charge you a third of normal prices. In fact, most charge about 60 per cent.

Not only that, but when the tax on booze rises in the budget, duty-free shops hike their prices too, even though no tax is being paid.

For this reason, gin, white rum and other drinks are often cheaper in foreign supermarkets than airport shops over here. So it's not sensible to buy and hump around airports bottles of spirit you might not normally drink anyway.

But try and strike up a friendship with any fellow passengers who do succumb to the temptation. They might need help later to put away their hastily bought holiday cheer. Perfume should be bought in airport shops rather than on planes, however, where prices are higher. You shouldn't, of course, fall into the trap of buying perfume or cigars to get a little bit off, if you wouldn't buy them normally anyway.

Some cameras and personal cassette-players have been found cheaper in British high streets than on duty-free counters. But never buy a camera or film abroad where they're even dearer.

## Holiday Money

It's usually best not to buy foreign notes here. Many countries give a better rate of exchange when you get there. And if you feel safe with cash have no truck with travellers' cheques. You pay twice – when you buy and when you exchange them. The company also enjoys the use of your money, interest free.

In any event, don't buy travellers' cheques until you check with your building society, or even your place of work. Sometimes they issue cheques or foreign currency without charging commission, unlike a bank or travel agent. Never order travellers' cheques in sterling. Ask for foreign denominations. Otherwise you pay more commission at the other end.

Your first job on arrival should be to note bank opening times. The hotel may conveniently cash your cheques at any time, but at a price.

Use credit cards abroad instead of travellers' cheques, if possible. There's no commission to pay, and British banks use a favourable tourist rate to work out how much you owe afterwards.

Wielding the plastic will stop you accidentally giving waiters too much in a strange currency. And you can use hole-in-the-wall machines to get foreign notes if you run short.

Your money will go further (psychologically) if you change small amounts. Your companions will also have to do most of the spending. This policy also minimizes pickpocket damage. The only good thing about these pests is that they're now so sophisticated that a money-belt no longer deters them. So you don't have to buy one.

## Eating Abroad

Apart from the ritzier watering holes, most restaurants serve the same stuff, bought from the same farmers and fishermen. Those places which aren't on the waterfront cut prices to compete with those that are. So eat in the side streets. You can always gaze at the harbour while taking a drink before and afterwards.

Back-street cafes have more of an ethnic atmosphere anyway. Happily for money-lovers, the run-down appearance of a holiday restaurant adds to the 'romance' of an Italian or Spanish night. A similarly appointed cafe in Rochdale evokes a more prosaic response.

Because of the sameness of fare, and uniformity of cooking quality in the average resort, once you've found a cheap place with a bit of life about it, you should stick with it. No doubt the flattered owner will see you eat well every night.

Before you finally choose this favourite restaurant, inquire where the locals eat, a sure sign of good cooking on the cheap.

## Buying Souvenirs

There are two rules about buying ethno-tat:

 Pause to ask yourself: 'Will this musical, plastic, illuminated gondola really look right on my mantelpiece in five years' time?'

If you still want it, haggle like crazy with the seller. The harder you try, the more you'll impress.

Street hawkers and beggars are a real pain in the foreign resort. See them off by memorizing the rudest way of saying 'Buzz off' in the local language. Your tormentor will scurry away in sheer surprise. You may, on the other hand, get a mouthful back, but at least no one will be trying to court your custom any more.

Another weapon to combat the street seller is to offer him your watch or camera at a very high price. As no one likes being made fun off, he will vanish. Faking madness has the same effect.

In some countries, traders actually try to pull you into shops. The counter-move is to stagger about while chortling incoherently. Storekeepers won't risk breakages by having a drunk on the premises.

## The Folks Back Home

Before leaving, put it about that you're not buying presents this year because, 'They're so rubbishy nowadays, aren't they?' Or tell friends, 'It would be a waste of time buying you anything from Costa Plonka. It wouldn't fit into a tasteful flat like this.'

## Guided Tours

Most excursions on travel company lists are poor value. They're seen as an easy way to make up the profit which was pared to make the package seem cheap in the first place.

Instead, approach a few fellow tourists. Suggest you hire a boat for the day from a local fisherman who could sail you around the coastline. As real life never matches up to fiction, you won't be shipwrecked or sold into slavery. But you will have a good laugh.

If you *do* end up on an official boat or coach excursion, it's useful to know that your guide is in league with the local business fraternity. That's why they enthuse so much over boring carpet factories or blown-glass industries. They're about to make 10 per cent commission on everything sold.

So if you really must laden yourself with a garish rug courtesy of child labour, tell your guide you will only buy if you can share her commission. If at first she demurs, raise your voice slightly so your friends and fellow countrymen can lend an ear.

## Hire Cars

Think thrice about hiring a car or motorcycle abroad. They're either expensive or cheap – the latter because they are falling to bits. All right, they may be insured, but would you fancy trying to sort out a claim a thousand miles away in a foreign language?

It's much more colourful and usually comical to share local buses with sheep and goats. And if you're ever in a hurry abroad, you're not in the holiday spirit anyway.

## How to Avoid Hotel Tipping

Anyone arriving in a hotel lobby is pounced upon by a spotty youth anxious to carry your bags. Tell him you're a scientist carrying a phial with a deadly virus inside.

Of course, there's always the danger he'll report your dangerous luggage to the manager. If this happens simply produce a paper file with notes on whooping cough inside.

You can avoid tipping someone who brings a room-service order by dashing into the bathroom, and running the shower.

Whenever you leave a hotel, you'll find a maid hanging round for a gratuity. Tell her you'll be back in a moment – and keep walking. Or leave a small coin in a very sturdy envelope, which will give you time to disappear before she manages to open it.

## Posh Hotels

Here's what to do if you find yourself in a tumbledown hotel with peeling paintwork, noisome guests and a sun-oil polluted swimming pool. Simply become a regular caller at the extremely pricey five-star establishment you're bound to find next door.

Relax by the better pool, and enjoy their luxury bars, toilets and phone booths. You are, after all, spending good money in their overpriced establishment, and making it look livelier than it might otherwise be.

It helps to make friends with a family who really are staying in the luxury hotel, so you can be seen with them. But, then again, the management can only ask you to leave.

This cuckoo-in-the-nest ploy is also useful for impressing gorgeous hunks and beautiful girls you've only just met.

## Cool Drinks

You can waste lots of pesetas and drachmas by forever leaping off the sand to buy small bottles of cool drinks. The cheap alternative is to fetch a large bottle of pop or fruit juice from a shop on the way to the beach and keep it propped up by stones on the sea's edge.

In fact, you'll keep more holiday money in your pocket by staying out of cafes and picnicking on bread, tomatoes, bananas *et al* from shops in the town.

## Making Amigos

Starting beautiful friendships is advisable in foreign holidays, especially with people from countries you've always wanted to see. One late night, full of international bonhomie, and pale ale, they may well invite you to visit them next year in the South of France, California or Bavaria.

They'll have forgotten you by the time you write to announce your imminent arrival, but by then it will be too late. It goes without saying that you should keep your own address to yourself, in case they have similar ideas.

Of course it's easier to strike up a friendship with fellow Britons. And if they live by the sea, near a national park, or somewhere like London or Edinburgh, you can work the same money-saving dodge.

The other advantage to ingratiating yourself with fellow holiday-makers is that you can ask their advice about the good value, or otherwise, of local restaurants, without making an expensive mistake yourself. And you can borrow their paperbacks, newspapers, cigarettes, flippers and inflatable seals.

If your new chums have hired a car, you can easily hitch lifts when they decide to try that new beach a few miles up the coast.

Other rewards can be won by getting to know an expatriate or, better still, a family of them. They'll want to show off their indolent new way of life, including the villa, the swimming pool, and perhaps even the yacht. You'll be lavishly entertained in return for your approbation and news of home.

These beneficiaries can be chatted up in those bars which imper-sonate British pubs, as they're driven there by home-sickness.

However, you should beware of that common pest in foreign bars – the Briton down on his luck. They look like those seedy characters portrayed by Denholm Elliott.

They'll ply you with unlikely local tales, as long as you buy the drinks all night. Understandable, of course, but a nuisance just the same. Tell them you left your money at home, for fast results.

## Free Nightlife

Unattached women should take advantage of any males steeped enough in the holiday spirit to buy the drinks. And men meeting young ladies can show their deep respect for sexual equality by letting them pay at the bar for a change. The most exotic, expensive cocktail should be ordered, especially if one's not bothered about seeing the buyer again.

Men will find it rewarding to air support for women's lib early in any holiday relationship. This leads to more understanding of your actions when you muscle into the lifeboat first, should a subsequent sea trip come to grief.

A weather eye should also be peeled for any wealthy loners who might be free with their money in exchange for a bit of holiday company.

## Coming Home

If you find yourself stuck with a purseful of coins in a foreign airport on the way home, don't rush about trying to spend them on things you don't want. While it's true that British banks won't exchange them when you get home, you can always deal with friends or colleagues who plan to visit the same country later on. You should also change any spare notes with them, too. Then you won't pay commission.

## HOLIDAYS IN BRITAIN

## Free Beds

The cheapest way to get away, especially with a young family, is to descend on friends or relatives. If they live by the sea or somewhere pretty, try to turn a fortnight's visit into an annual event.

If you put in a bit of effort over the year to keep in touch with all suitable targets, by making the odd phone call, say, there's no reason why you should ever have to pay for holiday accommodation again.

Flattery is the secret. If you keep saying, 'Your home should be

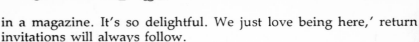

in a magazine. It's so delightful. We just love being here,' return invitations will always follow.

Should the hosts tend to get up your nose, time your visit only when they're working. This precludes bank-holiday weeks.

Mention in advance that you would quite like to see a show, and you may find the tickets are bought for you. But don't insult your hosts by bringing your own food.

On the same theme, you could arrange to swap homes for a fortnight with someone you know. This would give you much more freedom. And you won't have to worry about burglars or pets while you're away. Human nature being as it is, your home will probably be kept scrupulously clean.

Ask the owners of your temporary home to leave a list of free local entertainments and good pubs. Plunder their vegetable patch and fruit trees – but only if the produce was about to go off.

If you fancy a particular resort and don't know anyone there, you could advertise a house swap in the local paper. This, however, could be a bit risky.

People who own boats often issue holiday invitations to go sailing. These are welcome, until you realize they need sea-going labourers to do the crewing. The counter-move is to turn up, but to feign sea-sickness. All amateur sailors know you can't possibly work in that condition.

## Bed and Breakfast

Top hotels are clean, tidy, frequently unfriendly – and very costly. More modest hotels usually have the same disadvantages, minus the benefits. So why not pay just a fraction of hotel prices for bed and breakfast in an ordinary house. Or better still, an idyllic farmhouse on the outskirts of town.

I often choose those B and Bs near five-star hotels, so I can use the bar.

Contrary to popular belief, most B and B rooms are as clean and private as those in an hotel. They may be quieter at night. Owners take real pride in their breakfasts. The teapots aren't made of steel.

You won't have to pay the usual hotel premiums to use the phone. They may not be registered for VAT. And there's no one to tip.

Neither will you be expected to confirm bookings in writing or send a deposit.

Tourist offices list B and B houses. They'll ring up to check on vacancies. But all you really need do is cruise up and down a neighbourhood with large houses. Choose a smartly painted home with a manicured garden. The owners will be just as particular about the inside.

Just because this is a private house doesn't mean that, in the cause of politeness, you have to give up your rights. B and B providers are professionals too. Ask to see your room and don't shrink from inquiring about the price. They vary a lot.

If it seems too much, make your excuses, and leave. You could say, 'I wasn't expecting to stay in Mulchester overnight, and I haven't quite got that much.' They might offer an instant reduction.

Erring on the safe side, it's best not to offer to stay for more than one night in the first instance. If still satisfied next morning, you should ask, 'Is there a reduction if we stay another three or four days?'

Be charming and smile a lot when making suggestions like this. The proprietors may have a formal rule that no reductions are given. But they can break it more easily if the request is made informally. This is pop psychology at work.

## Hotels

If you are forced to stay in an hotel, ways of mitigating the financial damage are few. You can only avoid tipping (see page 125) and take full advantage of any freebies on offer.

Don't hesitate to pocket individual sachets of coffee, tea, sugar, shampoo, bubble bath, sewing sets and matches left in your room. You're paying for these as much as the bed. And there's no law that they must be used on the premises. Pocket the extras as soon as they appear. Replenishment will be made throughout the day.

To avoid any ill feeling, it is, perhaps, best to leave the cups dirty. This leaves the impression everything has been consumed *in situ*.

A tried and tested way of getting the best room available is to put Doctor, Professor, Lord or Lady before your name when confirming a reservation. This is legal as long as you don't make any money out of it. If the hotel management has a weakness for snobbery, then it's hardly your fault.

## Mobile Beds

The cost of overnight accommodation can be avoided if you buy a caravette: one of those big vans with beds and a sink. Buy one second-hand at an auction, or from a private owner. Like all used vans, they're cheap for their size.

You simply park on a caravan site, or anywhere without restrictions, preferably near a public convenience. As well as holidays, they're useful for courting purposes, scrounging furniture from relatives and working away from home. You can also hire them out to neighbours, if, that is, the insurance cover is satisfactory.

## The Camping Carry-on

Unless you are on safari, this isn't really the pursuit of a lady or gentleman. But if you must, borrow a tent – don't buy it. The owner will rarely have a use for it himself. You can also rent from camping shops. These may also sell second-hand tents which are getting too battered to hire out.

Camp sites are noisy and expensive. Ask a farmer if you can pitch in a field, instead. Play on sympathy. Tell him you had all your money stolen at the camp site you went to last night.

# Children

Do not discourage your children from hoarding, if they have a taste to it; whoever lays up his penny rather than part with it for a cake, at least is not the slave of gross appetite.

—*Samuel Johnson*

STARTING a family is a peerless way of knocking a big hole in your income. A salary may stop coming in altogether. Baby clothes, toys and pushchairs have to be bought, rooms redecorated. You'll be stuck with a big drain on your resources for two decades.

Though children learn more quickly at school nowadays, they still can't grasp that parental money doesn't grow on trees. So extra vigilance is needed to make sure you spend minimal amounts on your progeny.

Another problem is that your kids learn from you. Should you adopt the devious ways of living on others outlined in this book, you may well find Junior using some of the techniques on you. Be on your guard.

## Baby Clothes

Throw hints about baby's needs well before the birth. Then don't buy anything till all the presents have arrived from relatives, friends and workmates.

You may not have to buy much at all. But if you do, try those all-in-one suits which stretch to fit babies as they get bigger.

Casually mention any other needs to friends whose babies have just turned into toddlers. But don't pass any of *your* old baby clothes on, if you plan to enlarge your family.

## Prams, Cribs and Pushchairs

Scour the small ads and car boot sales for second-hand baby gear. Obviously, most things stay in passable condition, as they're outgrown very quickly. And so many parents are trying to dispose of prams, cribs and toys, there's a glut on the market. Expect to pay very little.

As usual when calling at a house to answer a small ad, appear in worn-out, patched clothing. This earns a more sympathetic response when haggling the price.

## Baby-sitting

Don't pay professionals. Get together with other parents and agree to help each other out. Lock the drinks cupboard.

## Toys

Fortunately for parents, expensive playthings are rarely what the younger child wants. The reason youngsters ignore the clockwork car in favour of its box is because they'd rather *do* something than *watch* a toy move around by itself. The box can be pulverized out of shape without Mum doing her nut.

This gives wide scope for making your own disposable toys from household waste – like cotton reels, washing-up bottles, cartons and string.

## Six Home-made Toy Ideas

A pile of old magazines and scissors can keep kids occupied for hours on end. You can turn this into a regular pastime, by adding a wallpaper sample book, doubling as a scrap-book. Flour in warm water makes an ideal paste.

Join two empty yoghurt containers with string, knotted through holes in the bottoms. The kids will enjoy a working walkie-talkie set, if the string is kept tight.

Smear Vaseline round a balloon. Dunk bits of newspaper in flour paste (see above) and stick them to the balloon. When dry, burst with a pin. Afterwards, parents can cut this globular creation into a light-shade.

Make hand puppets from old socks. Sew on buttons and bits of wool for eyes and hair.

If you can't be bothered with all this (and who could blame you), simply swap a box of toys with a neighbouring family for a week or so. Continue the process up and down the street.

Should your child makes a specific request for a rather costly birthday or Christmas present, act fast. Pass the request on to a doting aunt or uncle.

 Far faster and more exciting than a toboggan on the snow is an ordinary black bin-liner.

## Buying Second-hand

Many parents believe children don't take to used toys, as they're denied the fun of ripping off cellophane. This is a costly myth. Old junk, particularly mechanical gadgets once used by adults, and now recycled as junior play-things, are very acceptable.

The most diverting toy I ever had was a dilapidated wind-up gramophone bought for a pound. Though the best bit was standing on the revolving turntable, it lasted for ages.

I was also given an old clockwork train set, now worth a lot of money. Wish I knew where it went.

Old sporting equipment, from the attic or jumble sales, make excellent play-things. A battered tennis racket or ancient golf club will keep them out of your hair for weeks on end.

Ask older relatives to search cupboards for their old dolls, teddy bears and tin soldiers. Say, 'Young Mary would love to play with them.' When your child tires of these finds, sell them to antique shops which pay big money for ancient toys.

In all probability, none of your old play-things are still in one piece.

But if they are, inquire if they're now valuable before handing them over for destruction by the next generation.

You may well have some old books. So enthuse to your offspring about your childhood favourites, rather than modern ones. But don't hand over any volume until you've first read the back of the title-page. It might be a valuable first edition.

## New Toys

If you must buy toys, reject gimmicks in favour of traditional favourites. They never lose their amusement value. A kite is a good example. A cricket set another.

Never take children round toy shops. Don't give in to tears when they plead for something. Say they must wait for their birthday, or Christmas, then delegate the request to a relative.

A money-box is a fine present. It fosters more respect for your money.

## Free Garden Fun

Instead of investing in metal swings and slides, make sure your garden has apple trees. Their parallel branches are ideal for supporting home-made swings, and they're not too tall to climb (if you ban the higher reaches, that is).

Not only will young tummies be kept full in the autumn, but they'll stop your children turning to early crime by stealing fruit from somewhere else. And when tiny apples fall too early, youngsters have great fun chucking them at each other.

## Children's Parties

You may eventually be forced into this expensive ritual. You can easily make your own paper hats and place cards, but the price of all that food is daunting. One way of stemming the damage is to arrange the different cakes, trifles and jellies on separate tables or chairs.

Tell the guests that each food is in a different shop and, if they want it, they must pay in toy money. Distribute this 'money' sparingly, so they can't eat all that much. They'll enjoy themselves too much to realize they're still hungry.

## Music Lessons

Never force private music lessons on a child who doesn't want them. There's no such thing as an accomplished, but reluctant, musician.

When buying sheet music, you'll always find one copy which is dog-eared. This is because buyers like to thumb through scores to see if they're easy to play or not. You can ask for substantial reductions for slightly soiled music.

## Pocket Money

Youngsters should earn their pocket money. Give them regular jobs which might otherwise cost you money. Cleaning the downstairs windows, for example, or washing the car. Don't pay by the hour, of course, but for the completed job.

Take with a bag of salt those newspaper items which put pocket money averages at high levels. They're usually based on a small survey of children, not their parents. And youngsters will exaggerate their income as a boasting exercise. Set the levels of your children's pocket money at half those you read about.

When you're confronted by a junior trade unionist, try negotiation. Say you'll increase the allowance only if she watches less television, or the electricity bill goes down. This, you explain, is achieved by switching lights off.

## Young Entrepreneurs

You can ease the pressure for more pocket money by showing your children this list of profitable schemes:

Stage a backyard play, charging local kids to come in.

Hold a table-top sale of unwanted toys and comics outside the front gate. Sympathetic neighbours will buy anything.

Make a guy out of old clothes stuffed with newspapers and a mask. Round up some friends and exhibit from door to door in a push-chair. (This is more effective than hanging round street corners.)

Make home-made ginger beer, and barter it with school pals. Hint that it might be alcoholic.

Go carol-singing with a few extra touches to show you're professional. Arrange accompaniment on a violin or recorder. Carry a candle in a jam-jar on a broom handle.

Ask the corner shop to advertise your pet-sitting service for people on holiday. Specialize in rabbits, hamsters, guinea-pigs and goldfish. Leave cats and dogs to the professionals.

Banks and building societies offer young savers scores of 'freebies' to open an account, hoping they'll become customers for life. All your child has to do is to invest the minimum to walk off with piggy banks, toys, model banks and sports bags galore.

## Comic Relief

Send the kids to buy them in bundles at jumble sales. Or arrange a weekly swap – together with magazines for the adults – with other families nearby.

## School Trips

There's no doubting the horror of these. They're particularly expensive, because parents often subsidize scheming teachers who go free. It's hard to refuse your child when she tells you everybody else in the class is going to Russia or the Alps.

You could try lobbying the school governors to make the teachers stump up. This will stop any future trips. Otherwise all you can do is wait for Open Day to give the teachers concerned a dirty look.

## Cheap Thrills

The cost of many children's entertainments is extortionate. Never even consider the cinema, pantomimes, football matches, bowling alleys and pop concerts. Instead, exploit those traditional childish loves of watching animals and running amok outdoors.

A long walk along a river bank, a nature trail or through a local wood is ideal. Or a trip to an adventure playground in a council park.

A regional dog or cat show will go down well. Admission charges are nominal. But call towards the end and you won't be charged at all.

Youngsters like going to airports where planes can be admired taking off and landing from the visitors' lounge. Buy a second-hand metal detector (easy to find as the craze is over now).

Agree that once a pile of coins to the value of the purchase has been found, the kids can keep the machine. Then turn them loose on common ground. The acquisitive bent of most children is bound to get your money back safely.

Foster the reading habit in young children. Start with the *Beano* and work up to Tolstoy. Soon, a good book will stop them wanting to go out at all.

## Putting Children Off

If youngsters want to go to a zoo, or circus, remind them that Tarzan, Batman, or other childhood favourites would never approve of beautiful animals being caged up like that.

Should a fairground be preferred, recall that you read about three people falling off the big dipper the other week.

As children are hungry all the time, steer them away from all fast food centres. Admittedly this is very difficult in built-up areas nowadays.

So, if one such emporium does catch Junior's eye, casually mention a famous footballer or a celebrated film star whose career owes everything to scorning fatty foods like chips and beefburgers. Tell them they're very keen instead on egg and cress sandwiches. You happen to have some with you.

## Teenagers

Older children are a huge financial burden which can be partly alleviated by urging them to take a newspaper round, cafe work, baby-sitting job or similar part-time occupation. This will save you buying their clothes, make-up and CDs.

Keep complaining about your teenage children's unkempt look, thus making them even more determined to buy their attire from jumble sales. Or to patch up what they've got.

A strange custom of older children is to talk constantly during school hours only to ring each other up to continue this everlasting conversation at home. Offer to give your son or daughter a small sum every time a friend rings them first. Then you won't pay for the call.

Also, make it obvious you like listening in to private conversations. Teenagers do a lot of plotting against parents, so they'll bring calls to a speedy close if you hover about.

On no account have more than one phone. Then you can keep tabs on it.

Discourage teenagers from learning to drive. Lessons are dear, and if they pass they'll lose no time in borrowing your car and petrol. Even if you don't have to rectify bumps and scrapes, you'll still have a lot more mechanical wear to pay for.

If one of your tribe wants to go on holiday with a friend's family, don't object. But never subsidize someone else's teenager to come with you.

## Leaving the Nest

When your children want to leave home – let them.

# Social Occasions

Thrift, thrift, Horatio! the funeral baked meats
Did coldly furnish forth the marriage tables.
—*William Shakespeare*

FAMILY get-togethers like marriages, christenings, birthdays and anniversaries are cripplingly expensive. The following tips will ease the damage.

## A Marriage is Arranged

Paying for your daughter's wedding is one of the worst things to befall the dedicated frugalist. It's the third biggest expense you'll ever have thrust down your throat, next to your house and car. And there's nothing to show for it afterwards, except perhaps a few photographs, a shaky video, and a gown you won't be able to sell.

The event can be delayed, however, by praising every boyfriend your daughter brings home. She'll think there must be something funny about him. (Sons of millionaires are, of course, an exception, and should be the subject of blistering criticism.)

It's also worth acting strangely before each suitor, as nobody wants to import madness into the family.

When delaying tactics are exhausted, and a date is set, there are ways to defray the hideous cost, though special care is needed to make your parsimony undetected, if you're not to spoil your darling's big day.

Tell everyone that your daughter prefers a quiet wedding, whether she does or not. (It's fashionable to pretend you do, so she may string along.) In this way you can keep the guest list short, and avoid hiring top hat and morning coat.

On behalf of the couple, include on the guest list a lot of people who won't be able to come because they're in hospital, foreign countries, or aged 102. They'll still be expected to buy a present.

Borrow an etiquette book from the library and seek out any expenses which are traditionally met by the other parents. Tactfully suggest they meet their obligations.

Guests should be aware how to mitigate the inevitable expense to

138

them, too. If you're invited to a wedding some distance away, inquire if any fellow guests could give you a lift. Ask also if anyone can put you up. Explain: 'I've a recurring dream about dying in a hotel fire, so I don't like staying in one if I can help it.'

## The Reception

Hold it in your own home. If it's too small, a large tent can be hired for the garden. Persuade friends to do the catering.

If you arrange the wedding for 2 p.m., no one will expect a sit-down meal. You'll get away with a cold buffet. Announce sternly that you don't think children should drink champagne.

Every family has an uncle or aunt keen on cameras. Bestow on them the honour of official photographer. With a bit of luck a guest will own a video camera, too.

## Wedding Gifts

Wrap up something of little value. Omit to put your name on the parcel. As other guests will genuinely forget to identify their gift, or the happy couple get all their presents mixed up after unwrapping them, your adroitness will never be discovered. Confirmation of this comes when you get an all-purpose 'thank-you' letter.

Alternatively, come with a crumpled piece of gift wrapping, attached to a gift tag with your name on it. After the opening ceremony, leave this on the floor with other wrappings. The couple will doubtless find the paper later, but will be too embarrassed to tell you they've already mislaid your non-existent gift.

The newly marrieds should carefully store any unwanted gifts still in their cartons and gift paper, ready for the next time they become guests at a wedding.

## Births

It's customary to give newly borns a present. Try searching out a family heirloom you never really liked, a pair of ebony elephants perhaps, and say, 'I know Aunt Agatha would have liked baby to have this. It's been in the family for so long.'

Or tell the proud parents, 'I'm not going to give your little son a present now. Let's wait till he can appreciate it.' Sadly, your memory lets you down.

## Divorce

Keep solicitors out of it at all costs. If there are no children involved, you won't need one – as long as you don't begin fighting. Get a form from the county court, fill it in and pay the small fee.

## Funerals

Don't couch your condolences in a telegram, a short note is enough. A simple bunch of flowers from your own garden is often more acceptable than a commercial wreath. Or offer to go halves in a floral tribute with a mutual relative or friend.

## Hospital Visiting

Don't patronize those flower shops which grow up around all large hospitals. If you live in the same house as the patient, take them one of their own houseplants, preferably one in flower, and say earnestly, 'I though this would remind you of home.'

If the sufferer is about to undergo an operation, take chocolates. They won't be allowed to eat them, and you can bring them home.

## Birthdays

Keep your birthday gift list very short. Cross off names at the slightest excuse. Children can legitimately be struck off on leaving school.

The cheapness of a present can be disguised by saying, 'I want you to take care of this, because, though it might not look it, it did cost rather a lot of money.'

Carefully save all useless presents sent to yourself for recycling later. Keep a list so the giver doesn't get the same thing back.

Buy all your birthday presents at the same time: the January sales.

If your birthday card is appropriate to the recipient, its apparent cheapness won't matter. So scan market stalls for inexpensive golfing cards, if dad is a golfer, or football cards if your nephew is a soccer fanatic. Cards with cartoon characters who happen to look like Aunt Jo or Uncle Ian are also worth hoarding.

## Season's Greetings

Let's see how you can whittle away your Christmas card bill to next to nothing. Begin by buying them in January when they're half price or less. (You'll also get amazing bargains in wrapping paper, tree lights, Santa Claus mugs and decorations.)

Cut down your sending list by half. People who normally get a card from you will take exactly one year, or perhaps two, to stop sending one to you. This is inconvenient. People who are successful have to be seen to receive more cards than most. But the deficiency can be made up by saving all your old cards. Then put them up again with the new batch. Stick the old ones on a ribbon, high on the wall, where nobody can read them and find you out.

You'll be considered both artistic and thoughtful if you make your own cards. Simply fold coloured card in half. Use a plastic stencil and a child's watercolour set to create snowmen, robins, fir trees and reindeer. Keep it simple. Sprinkle the wet paint with glitter. Better still, get the kids to do it.

When you send cards to a branch of the family living in one town, despatch them all in the same envelope to one address. (It's wise not to take this course if several family members live near you. You could also receive a wad of cards to deliver by hand.)

If you get a card from someone with the same Christian name as yourself in which is written 'from Liz' and nothing else, you can post it on to another friend as one of your own cards. Simply stick another label on the envelope.

Another dodge on the same theme is to doctor a card from Janet and John, say, by adding 'and of course Liz' in the same ink. Then you can remail the card to a mutual friend.

People you never see, but who keep sending you a card year after year, can be put off for good by writing 'not known at this address' on the envelope. Then put it in a pillar box.

Be wary of charity cards. Though these are often highly priced, sometimes only a small percentage goes to the good cause. Consider sending a small donation directly to the charity, instead.

## Christmas Presents

Early in the year, agree on a price limit for gifts with everyone on your list. They'll have forgotten all about the contract by December. But you won't.

Take early cuttings from your houseplants which flower at Christmas. They'll grow to an acceptable size by December. This works best for friends who've admired the mother plant in the past.

Never post presents. Deliver them by hand when you happen to be passing – even if that's two months too early. An early gift is perceived as 'thoughtful'.

Ignore tradition. Open each present as soon as you get it. Then you can immediately resend it to somebody who doesn't know the original giver. Open with precision, and you can even use the same paper.

As it's now socially responsible to reuse all wrapping paper, take a medium hot iron and smooth it out from the unprinted side. Save on paper (and postage) by not buying bulky presents. Cut up old cards to make gift tags.

Give the children modest stockings to put out, not pillow cases.

## Christmas Trees

Artificial trees are more acceptable in these days of woodland conservation. But if you must spend every year on a real one, it's cheaper (and traditionally correct) to buy in the last week before Christmas. As your central heating won't have ravaged the leaves as much, the tree will be fresh right up to Twelfth Night.

Buy from those traders who deal from a truck in the street, or from a market stall, rather than greengrocers. Go late in the day when they've started to visualize a load of useless trees on their hands after Christmas. Haggle without mercy.

Cheap straggly trees can be made bushier by tying on spare branches always found lying around Yuletide vendors. You can also have a chunky, shapely tree by binding two poorly clad specimens together. Double-stemmed firs are found in the wild.

Two short trees can be lashed into one larger one in the same way, the join being hidden under tinsel. A modest tree can also appear taller by standing it on a pile of bricks inside a container like a small barrel.

Summer boot sales are a rich source of used decorations, in more interesting old-fashioned designs. You often find used baubles and tinsel poking out of dustbins after Christmas. And look for them in the attic. Someone, who owned the house before you, may have forgotten putting them there.

Tree ornaments are easy to make:

> Dab fir cones with white or silver paint.

> Paste Victorian characters, robins and snowmen from old Christmas cards and magazines onto cardboard, cut them out and suspend from thread.

> Cut cardboard into stars and cover in cooking foil.

If all this sounds like hard work, ring up your child's teacher (or acquaintances in the profession) and suggest the ideas are taken up in the art class. Make sure the results are brought home.

## Ways to Deal with Carol Singers

 Before Christmas, move into the back room and put all the front lights off.

Attach a note to the door saying, 'Dear Dave, just popped out to Lucy's for a bit. Let yourself in.'

Shout out, 'Come back nearer Christmas.'

If they return in Christmas week yell, 'I'm sorry, but I've had a lot of carol singers already and there's no money left, now.'

Make ghostly moaning noises in the hall.

Stage a noisy family row. Continue unabated after the knock on the door.

Rush out of the front door in mid-carol, yelling 'Look out, he's got a gun.'

Pretend the door is stuck.

 Pin a postcard to the door, proclaiming, 'Danger! Subsiding Porch!'

## A Seasonal Warning

Avoid the postman and milkman in the week before Christmas, but it's risky not to tip the dustmen. Their memories are twelve months long exactly. They may refuse to take bulky items during this period, fail to replace your lid, and decorate your drive with tea-bags and bean tins.

Your only chance is to leave your dustbins empty for two weeks before Christmas, giving the impression that you've gone away. Leave your rubbish in bin-liners by the dustbins next door.

## Easter

The confectionery industry admits that, as far as they're concerned, Easter eggs wouldn't be Easter eggs without the over-packaging. If you want to avoid paying for that, buy chocolate bars for the kids, and revive the tradition of painting their own hard-boiled eggs. It's more fun, anyway.

## Valentine's Day

Most cards are unsigned, so you can recycle them next year. Buy a very cheap card, if you need another envelope.

## Mother's Day

Again, something from the garden is more personal than chocolates or bought flowers. Father's Day – unless, of course, you're a father yourself – should be dismissed as a cynical commercial gimmick. I once tried to introduce a Son's Day, by the way. It didn't work.

# Pets

If you spend a thing you can not have it.
(Non tibi illud apparere si sumas potest.)
—*Plautus*

IT'S cheaper (and kinder) to buy humane mousetraps than cats. Burglar alarms are cheaper than dogs, too. But if you must have either, follow these money-saving rules:

 Start kittens on the cheapest tinned food going. Let them have just one sniff of the dearer brands and they'll ignore every other variety for life.

Make tins go further by mixing in the cheaper, dry crunchy foods. Pets' teeth last longer that way, too.

Going on holiday? Don't throw money at kennels and catteries. Ask neighbours to look after your dog. It will be spoilt rotten, and may not want to return. Cats are happier staying at home. Trust your keys with a young neighbour to keep them fed.

Use sand rather than pricey cat litter.

Only insure your pet against vets' fees in the second half of its life, when risk of illness is greater.

Try to make your vet think you can't afford big fees. Don't let her see your pet in an expensive carrying basket. Use a battered cardboard box or plastic bag instead. Wear old clothes to the surgery. Say things like, 'Oh dear, Tiddles, I don't know what we're going to do if you're poorly again.' Vets are soft-hearted. It's an important part of the job. If you look destitute she's more likely to charge less, or perhaps waive the fee altogether. Being a vet, she can afford to.

After treating your pet, vets invariably ask you to bring it back next week. Ostensibly, this is to check on progress, but really it could be to charge another fee. Forestall this move on your return by saying accusingly, 'Your treatment didn't work. It wasn't cheap, so what are you going to do to put it right?' I also have it on good authority that you won't have to pay any grasping vet for expensive worming treatments if you hide occasional pieces of raw garlic in your pet's food.

Don't buy a rabbit, white rat, guinea-pig, tortoise, hamster or gerbil. Put a card in a shop window offering a free home to anyone who's recently grown out of small pets like these.

Waste no money on cat toys, like fluffy mice and balls with bells inside. Feline fancy is more likely to be attracted to a bit of rag on a string or a selection of cardboard boxes left on the lawn. For hours of free doggy fun, an old slipper is best.

Ask the butcher or fishmonger for food scraps. Better still, send your children in – but first rehearse with them a special forlorn look.

# Auctions, Flea Markets and Boot Sales

What piles of wealth hath he accumulated
To his own portion! . . . How, i' the name of thrift
Does he rake this together?
                                    —*William Shakespeare*

BUYING at auctions is such a profitable way of saving money that it deserves most of a chapter of its own. Not only are salerooms brimming with furniture, but all kinds of household implements can be yours for a fraction of shop prices. It's not at all unusual to see an electrical job lot of toaster, iron and kettle all knocked down for a few pounds. They could well be current models, still selling in the high street. Such a purchase would make your money go an incredible thirty times as far.

Collections of garden tools are commonly disposed of at give-away prices. And old spades won't bend the minute you dig in. Colour TVs change hands very cheaply, too. They're usually switched on so you can check the picture.

You'll have gathered that I'm not talking about top London auction houses, but modest suburban ones. For some reason, weekly auctions aren't always well advertised in local papers – a big advantage for buyers – but all salerooms are listed in the yellow pages.

The main disadvantage to buying at auction is that choice is limited. You may have to make several visits before you find what you want. But, if you make a regular habit of attending a weekly auction, you may never have to buy anything new again. Eventually everything is sold there. And I mean everything.

To save wasting time attending an unsuitable auction, ring up and ask about what they've got. Every extra punter improves the prices – and their commission – so you'll find staff very helpful.

The hidden bonus of urban auction houses is that, all too often, the man with the hammer doesn't know what he's talking about. Contrary to popular belief, no qualifications are necessary. As vendors are equally clueless about the value of auntie's old clock or mother's 'hideous' vase, you can see the advantage. I once saw an admittedly unattractive painting by a particularly famous artist go for just a few hundred pounds. It's possible the buyer may have no need to work again.

## *How to Tell an Ignorant Auctioneer*

If he says 'Here's an unusual piece,' and you've seen several of them before.

Many antiques have French names, e.g. pince-nez spectacles and Famille Rose porcelain. An auctioneer who mispronounces these words doesn't know his stuff.

If he describes an antique as 'period' or says 'this has a bit of age to it', then he doesn't know how old it is. If he describes the piece as Georgian, Victorian or Edwardian, he's a bit more informed. But a competent auctioneer will give an approximate date.

If he misses bids, he's probably new to the job.

Inexperienced auctioneers haven't yet gained the confidence to tell jokes.

## *Know Your Auction Rights*

You have less rights at an auction sale than you do in a shop. The radio set you bought doesn't have to be working, unless it says so in the catalogue. A flower vase need not hold water, unless it was stated to be in first-class condition. The firm doesn't have to draw attention to imperfections. Catalogues are often short on detail for this very reason.

Be very suspicious if the initials A.F. or A.S. appear after a catalogue entry. They mean 'as found' or 'as seen'. The item is therefore incomplete, cracked or defunct.

Other expressions like 'thought to be' and 'in the style of' are also handy get-out clauses for auction houses.

If a catalogue describes something as Georgian, and it turns out to be of this century, then they have to refund your money. Even if your purchase is George VI. Threaten them with the Fraud Squad.

You should also be aware that many salerooms expect you to pay a buyer's premium, usually 10 per cent, on your bill. You also have to pay Value Added Tax if the seller is VAT registered.

Beware the 'cloaking' technique. It works like this. Dealers who spot something they like, loom over it during the sale. This hides it from others with the same taste. If it's a chair, stool, or something robust, like a table or a sideboard, they sit on it. It's not unknown for traders to wear a voluminous overcoat, even in summer, to help the hiding process.

Saleroom staff often turn to the wall articles with cracks or bits missing, to hide the defects. If you'd still like to buy such an item, turn it round, just before the sale, so other bidders will clearly see the problem. They'll be put off.

Never be the first to bid. The price might drop a lot more before anyone puts their hand up. If the piece is knocked down as 'unsold' because the auctioneer can't get a bid, you can always shout out that you'd like the piece to be put up again. And if that fails, you can make your offer in the office after the sale.

When the auctioneer puts up an unusual item which you fancy (unusual stuff is worth more), you should giggle loudly. This makes rivals feel ridiculous if they join in the bidding. This works particularly well for nude pictures and erotic items.

Similarly, if the auctioneer suggests an opening price for the item you've set your heart on, snort sardonically. This will signal to those around you that the suggested price is far too high. They may also get the wrong impression that this lot is a fake.

One should draw the line, though, at a very dirty, not to say dishonest, trick used by some dealers. This involves switching lot numbers by interfering with labels on pieces of furniture. This means they'll get a bargain, while somebody else definitely won't.

## How to Avoid Getting Stung

Unscrupulous auctioneers will 'run you up' by taking bids 'off the wall'. This is what happens. You offer £10 for a washing machine. The auctioneer looks towards the back of the room and takes a 'bid' for £12. You put your hand up for £15. This could go on for some time. But in reality, there is no other bidder – and you've lost a lot of money.

The counter-move is to peer behind you querulously in a conspicuous fashion. If your rival bidder is a phantom, the auctioneer will quickly knock the lot down to you.

Another illegal practice you may have heard about is the operation of a ring. This involves dealers entering into a conspiracy not to bid against each other. They later sell the items privately between themselves. But this won't harm you if you're buying. Only sellers are hurt by ringing.

Beware of Victorian oil paintings of pretty chocolate-box subjects, especially children or animals. There's now a roaring trade in copying old prints of appealing subjects and putting the result in battered frames. Many of these fakes are executed by talented child labour in the Far East.

A lot of modern Chinese pottery is smeared in brown grease and rolled in grime to make it look as ancient as the Ming Dynasty. Remember that people selling real antiques will have carefully cleaned them before the sale.

Watch out for silver objects. Unless the catalogue describes them as hall-marked or HM, the precious metal content may be so diluted they may not be worth very much.

Reproduction furniture is often 'distressed'. That means banged about with a hammer to make it look old. Feel around for rough edges. Genuinely old pieces will have had many years to be rubbed smooth.

Fake antiques have flooded the market in recent years: Chinese vases, stewardship ornaments, and pistols. If the ever-present dealers aren't buying, avoid these items too.

## Seasonal Bidding

There are good and bad times to buy at auction. July and August sales produce the best bargains, because many regular bidders are away on holiday, so competition is weak. January and February are almost as good. Attendances are down then because people are still short of money after the expense of Christmas.

On the other hand, it's not wise to buy – though it's a good idea to sell – in November and December. That's when dealers do battle with each other, as they try to keep their shops well stocked for Christmas.

Incidentally, auction houses are ideal places to buy Yule gifts, especially bankrupt stock still in its packaging. But you should bid in the summer.

An easy way to make money is to buy jewellery in June and July. Then put it back in the auction for resale just before Christmas. Many dealers get into a late panic then, as they hunt for something personal to give their wives and husbands. Their usual stingy tendencies are forgotten in the heat of desperate competition. You could get an exaggerated price for your ring or necklace.

## Selling at Auctions

If you want to raise money from a poor-quality painting, ask the saleroom to hang it high, at the back of the room. Only the eagle-eyed can recognize lack of artistic talent from a distance.

Real antiques should be well cleaned before you take them to the auction. Few salerooms will do it for you. Items from this century should be left covered in grime and dust to make them more interesting.

Don't sell small items in individual lots. You'll pay a 'handling charge' and insurance for each. Pour everything into a box to sell as a job lot. Arrange the best bits on top.

## How to Buy at Flea Markets and Boot Sales

A weekly trip to a large flea market or car boot sale is a necessity for any serious money-saver. Everything that costs pounds in the shops now changes hands for pence in the fields and car parks of Britain.

Motorists acquire car jacks and tyres for next to nothing. Parents find toys. The potting of plants and the concocting of jams are once again cottage industries. Cooking apples, potatoes, kindling wood, broom handles are all there, for next to nothing.

Long-playing records are good buys at boot sales. Most are in surprisingly good condition. If they're discarded, they can hardly be favourite records. So they haven't been played much. Some vintage records, and a lot of newer ones, can make big money now. Particularly watch out for rock-'n'-roll discs from the fifties.

Forget about those expensive picture-framing shops in the high street. A boot sale has a stunning choice of suitable frames for your own artistic efforts or ancient sepia portraits of Great Aunt Maude. You don't need skill to reframe a picture – just a pair of scissors and a reel of sticky tape.

Gilt frames are much cheaper if they're chipped, revealing the white plasterwork underneath. This often happens to pictures carted to and from boot sales every week. They can be restored in minutes though by buying a pot of artificial gilt from art shops and smearing it over the chip.

You can also revitalize your jaded possessions, without having to purchase new ones, if you scour the stalls. Vital spare parts, like electric kettle leads, bicycle saddles and teapot lids are all there for the taking.

But don't buy anything that isn't working. Despite what the stall holder might say, a silent transistor radio or an immobile watch is never worth the cost of repair, even if the broken components are still available.

Always visit flea markets towards packing-up time. Stall holders, frustrated at having sold little all day, will want to save face by selling something at all costs. Your 'silly' offer will stand a bigger chance of being accepted.

Train your children to ask for small toys, and then to throw a tantrum when you say you can't afford it. 'Car-booters' are a soft-hearted breed who often give things away to tearful children.

## How Some Dealers Sell at Flea Markets

They fold old linen carefully to hide rents, darns and evidence of moths.

They stick a price ticket over any blemishes on ornaments.

Selling a stack of plates? They put the cracked one at the bottom.

An untidy jumble on a stall looks more interesting than carefully laying out stock like a row of soldiers.

They arrange for an accomplice to keep coming round saying, 'That clock's very cheap. One just like that sold for £905 in Ramsbottom's only last week.'

If someone asks the date of something which looks old, but they know to be fairly recent, they pretend to be French.

They put fragile things that are not likely to sell near the front edge of the stall. Visitors may knock them over and break them. Then they can politely suggest that some compensation is in order.

The very best spot to occupy at a boot sale is the third table, nearest the entrance, on the left-hand side. People usually tour in a clockwise direction. Their eyes don't usually focus until they've passed two stalls. And after the third stall their interest gradually begins to wane.

# Making Easy Money

Saving is getting.
—*Giovanni Torriano*

THOUGH this book is really about saving money, it's also about having money. So it's worth including a few ways of improving your income. Without hard work, of course.

## Small Claims Courts

If anyone offends you – the dry-cleaners leave a stain on your best evening gown, or a runaway lorry crashes through your washing – sue them. Take out a special form in the local county court for a very small fee. There are no court costs, and you can be your own solicitor.

You can only claim up to £500, but that can work in your favour. Often, the firm won't bother to contest your claim. (They may be frightened of publicity.)

I know of someone who successfully sued a newspaper for £200 because they failed to publish an advertisement to sell his car on the due date. He'd taken a wasted day off work to deal with potential buyers who never came.

## Game Shows

Down-market TV game shows are so embarrassingly awful that most intelligent people refuse to appear in them. So the competition is weak and all the questions have to be childishly easy. I recently saw one contestant, with the confidence to answer general knowledge questions before millions, answer that the Elgin marbles are used to play a game in Scottish school playgrounds.

If you can put up with a bit of torture for half an hour, it's well worth writing to TV companies for an entry form. You can sell any unwanted prizes to retailers. Or ask the game show organizers to give you the money instead and recycle the prizes for next time.

## Home Produce

It's the easiest thing in the world to grow fruit and vegetables, and put a cardboard sign on the front gate. Merely wait for customers at the door when you're in and take it down when you go out.

People calling at a house are much more polite than they are in shops. And they're embarrassed to leave without buying anything.

If you have children, set them up with a table inside the front gate. Though they'll demand a share of the profits, a child's stall is appealing enough to counter this expense.

Only sell stuff which grows itself in great numbers. These include potatoes, runner beans, sprouts, courgettes and carrots. You may have a surplus of apples and pears, too. Easily propagated indoor plants, like spider plants, can be added to your stock.

Casually say to customers buying a sack of spuds that they ought to have some spider plants as they absorb harmful carbon monoxide (which they do).

Sell in bulk, by the sackful, to save the expense of buying scales. Check prices of local farms who sell by the roadside, then undercut them.

As you haven't been daft enough to waste money on chemical fertilizers, you can truthfully advertise your produce as 'organic'. This really pulls 'em in. (You may need council consent to sell like this.)

## Free Market Stalls

If you arrive at lunchtime at a market, preferably on a chilly day, you'll find traders packing up early. Ask if you can take over their stall for the afternoon. Plonk your garden stuff or household white elephants on it. And off you go.

## Emergency Beds

Providing bed and breakfast formally is hard work. But you can make pin money by leaving your address at the local pub. When they get full, they can send guests to you. The punters won't expect a sterling service, if you explain you're only coming to the rescue in an emergency, out of the goodness of your heart.

## It's All in a Name

Keep a posh autograph book in your car. If you spot a famous person signing books or opening a supermarket, or simply walking in the street, get them to sign it. Some of the names I've collected in this way – including Sir Henry Moore and Bing Crosby – are worth money.

## Order of the Boot Sale

It used to be unthinkable to be seen selling your worldly goods in a field somewhere, but not any more. Collect up your rubbish and take it down to the nearest sale advertised in the local paper. You don't have to book a space, though it's a bit cheaper if you do.

Take a folding table – a wallpaper pasting table will do – and an old velvet curtain to put over it.

You will make more money than you think, and will come away amazed at what some folk buy.

Also staggering is the amount of ignorance shown by fellow stall holders. Search out those antiques which are totally undervalued by their owners. Buy them and make money by putting them in auctions.

A lightning seller at boot sales are, surprisingly, garden gnomes, sold for their 'kitsch' value. All you need is a couple of rubber moulds, a big bag of plaster of paris, and paint remains from the shed. Charge healthy prices. You'll get them.

## Under the Hammer

Buy jewellery, prints and other likely Christmas presents at sale-rooms in the spring when others are saving for their holidays. Or in July and August when attendances are thin because people are already on holiday. Then put the stuff back in the auction at the beginning of December. You will double or treble your outlay.

Another good way to make money at auctions is to buy furniture covered in paint, have it stripped professionally, and then put it back in.

## House Search

Executives who are relocated to different parts of the country have to find a new home quickly. Usually they're too busy to spend the huge amounts of time demanded by the quest.

Come to the rescue. Write to the personnel officers of any large concerns setting up in your area. Say that if anyone sends a list of requirements, you'll find their ideal home for a small commission. Then take the list round local estate agents.

## A Good Bet

A good way of making money – and having a good laugh – is by betting a friend that you can do something or other he can't. The best place for this is the pub or at a party where there are witnesses. Your friend will lose face if he isn't a good sport.

Here are two examples that never fail:

'I bet you £5 you can't write a small letter i with a small dot over it.'

Your friend will write the normal dotted i. You point out that it should have two dots over it to fit the description.

'I bet you £5 you can't button up your coat in less than a minute.'

When this is achieved in less than a minute, you point out that he buttoned *down* the coat by beginning at the top.

## Christmas Greenery

If you have a holly tree in your garden, cut bits off, bundle it up and hawk it around local greengrocers and market stalls. They'll buy it from you. You may also find more lucrative mistletoe. It grows on oaks and other trees.

Christmas wreaths are a money spinner, too. Make a circle of bendy twigs. Wind ivy around this creation, and work pieces of holly in.

## *Photomania*

Scour junk shops for old postcards of street scenes, pubs, hotels, shops, and stately homes. They may not be very interesting to you, but they'll be fascinating glimpses of the past for present-day owners of these properties. Write to their addresses offering your postcard. Say you've had it framed and blown up by a photographer. If they bite you can get this done later very quickly. You could command a very high price for such a rare desirable item (to them).

# How to be Thought of as Green, not Mean

There is more art in saving than in gaining.
*—German Proverb*

NOT too long ago people who doggedly tried to save money were derided as stingy. Those who read by the window in the dying light of day, to delay switching on the light, were laughed at. Anybody reusing an old envelope was treated with disdain.

At the same time, waste was seen as a healthy part of progress. Electricity boards relied on adverts of scantily dressed families prancing around in mid-winter with central heating turned to maximum. No car manufacturer dreamed he could sell more of his latest model by making it use less petrol. Having the wherewithal to squander the earth's resources was fashionable, a sure sign of affluence, a success signal.

Fortunately for those of us who respect money, public opinion has made a dramatic U-turn. People who save, reuse and spend very little are now respected. Anyone poking around in a skip or turning over woollens at jumble sales is a shining example in the Caring Nineties.

At last, we can retrieve discarded newspapers from public litter bins without attracting a pitying look. One is, after all, saving rain forests.

Suddenly, lots of the things we did secretly to save cash can now be practised with pride. It's known as the 'Green Have Effect'.

And this chapter is devoted to ways you can appear to be improving the environment for the benefit of all, while secretly working to feather your own nest.

## How to Let Friends Know You've Gone Green

Even if you think planet-saving is a load of twaddle, you first need to convince people you've seen the light about wasting earthly resources. One method is to go round making gentle remarks about what people eat, or pour down the sink. Another is to wear a tin badge for a week or two saying 'One Green World' or 'Working for the Environment'.

Alternatively, bring a coffee mug to work inscribed with another suitably green slogan, like 'Rats Have Rights, Too'. This sort of thing comes from market stalls run by bearded enthusiasts.

## Ten Green Excuses for Saving Money on Food

Remind members of your family who're prone to leaving food on the plate that fifteen million children starve to death every year.

Grow your own fruit and veg without using chemical fertilizers and insecticides. You'll no longer be regarded as a crank, and sent a smock for Christmas.

Shun over-packaged food. It's always dearer, and it's bad for dwindling South American forests which supply the extra cardboard and paper.

Emotionally blackmail your loved ones into becoming vegetarians. You can, of course, secretly continue to eat meat yourself. Explain that 10 lbs of grain is needed to fatten cows to produce one 1 lb of beef and that livestock and poultry are often kept in barbarous conditions. Many sows are kept tethered round the neck and girth all their lives. This limits their exercise making them profitably fat for the market.

Collect lurid leaflets from animal rights campaigners to back up your arguments. Add that cows, sheep and pigs also produce methane, one of the worst greenhouse gases.

If a lot of tea is knocked back in your home as a relaxing drink, remind everyone in the family that most varieties contain some caffeine, which is a stimulant. Hastily add that it's no good changing to coffee as a cup of that will often contain up to twice as much caffeine as your average cuppa.

In any event, buy loose tea. This costs half as much as tea-bags, which are made of bleached paper and chemicals, including formaldehyde.

Steer clear of health shops. They can be expensive, and some of their wares, like honey, aren't particularly good for you.

Tinned food isn't the cheapest way of eating meat, fruit or vegetables. Stop buying cans on the grounds that the smelting plants used to process them cause pollution. Transporting tinned food also wastes petrol because it's heavy to move around.

Learn to sneer at the description 'juice drink' on the cartons of fruit juice. Some of these confections contain only 20 per cent of the fruit. Yet they can cost as much as the real thing. Buy only 100 per cent juices – known as 'pure' – and dilute them to taste.

Mini-cartons of juice, sold mainly for the lunchtime trade, take a lot of energy and cardboard to make. So they cost up to four times as much as buying your juice in normal 1-litre cartons. Boycott them.

Most cocoa beans are treated with pesticides. Instead of chocolate treats, buy the kids natural liquorice roots to chew on. You save your cash. They save their nashers.

## How Green is Your Valet?

People who declare themselves friends of the earth – even if they don't mean it – now have the excuse not to lash out on new expensive leather and suede coats. This is a big relief.

However, we can still search out second-hand versions. 'The poor animal is long gone, and I hate waste' is the correct approach here.

When haggling for a used leather coat, persuade the trader that hardly anyone wants skins nowadays. 'Skin' sounds more disgusting than leather.

Until recently, women who needed to look wealthy sported fur coats. But any wearers of mink, sable and leopard now are considered to be barbarian. This turnabout is a boon to husbands and boyfriends.

Crocodile handbags and snakeskin bags – once the height of extravagance – are also looked down on nowadays, too.

When it comes to the expensive business of keeping clothes clean, there are lots of green savings to be made. Give a wide berth to stain removers, whose chemicals get into the water chain. Instead, give the soiled garment a good scrub with soap before putting it in the wash.

Dry-cleaning is not only expensive, but some of the solvents change the ozone layer. The formaldehyde used in many processes gives off fumes for weeks after your skirt comes back from the cleaners. Beware the 'dry-clean only' label when shopping.

Be sceptical about the idea that clothes which are frequently washed last longer because abrasive grit is removed. This is put about by washing machine manufacturers and detergent makers. Common sense dictates that over-washing will wear things out.

## Energy

One of the most effective ways of preserving the planet while preserving your funds is to reduce household heating. Using one therm of gas makes five kilograms of the greenhouse gas, carbon monoxide. Electricity produces this nuisance, too.

We've dealt with energy savers earlier in this book. Here are a few more:

 Use a kettle that will boil only the amount of water it takes for one cup of tea. Use small saucepans, then you won't waste energy heating up a large expanse of metal. Take any sliding trays you don't need out of cookers.

Wash up in cold water. It doesn't need scalding temperatures to shift grease; that's what washing-up liquid is for.

Cut vegetables into small pieces when cooking. It takes half the time. Boil different vegetables in the same pan.

Ordinary light bulbs create carbon dioxide, a greenhouse gas. Use fluorescent bulbs. They cost more but eventually save by lasting longer, and using a quarter of the power.

Tell family members and lodgers that you are cutting an hour from the daily 'central heating time' to save on precious resources at the power station. Pick a time when you're usually out.

## Green Cleaning

A lot of noxious chemicals go down plug holes, to attack the environment. Don't buy any more bath cleaners and scouring creams. Use borax (from chemists) to deal with sinks, baths and surfaces.

Blue toilet blocks aren't really much good. They do kill microbes, but they also see off the natural organisms which would despatch the germs anyway.

Don't buy chemicals to unblock sinks. If these concoctions can cut through gunge, think what they might do when drained away into the natural world. Pipes can be cleared with washing soda crystals.

A rolled-up newspaper is cheaper than fly-sprays which contain chemicals that harm pond life and bees. Keep your home free of food remains and they won't be around to swat anyway.

There's always a cheaper way of buying something than in an aerosol. Your green excuse for avoiding them is that even those spray cans with no CFCs, often optimistically marked as ozone-friendly, may have other polluting gases in them.

Forego kitchen rolls. Not only does the paper use up trees, but it's bleached with chemicals. Eventually this paper ends up on rubbish tips where rain carries it into the waterways. Tear up old clothing to wipe away kitchen mishaps.

Detergents for dishwashers are pricey. Some are tested on animals. Use a half-and-half mixture of borax and baking soda instead.

You'll save cash, and stop polluting the atmosphere, by buffing up furniture with olive oil, instead of an aerosol of chemical polish.

Use paint on your walls instead of paper. It's cheaper. And if we all did it, South American forests would last longer. Stencils make painted surfaces more interesting.

## A Green Bill of Health

Nearly all drugs have side effects, even some mild ones sold without a prescription. Yet there's probably no need to buy most of the remedies sold without a doctor's note at the chemist.

If you suspect you're ill you should of course see a doctor. But if you have an ordinary cold, cough, sore throat or headache, think twice about parting with your money.

Even your GP may only prescribe tablets because she thinks you expect it of her. Ask if a drug is really necessary. It's you who has to pay the prescription charge!

There is no cure for a cold so why try to fight it? All pushy pharmaceutical companies can offer you are preparations which 'comfort' the symptoms. The best 'comforter' for a cold is the thought that you can use it as an excuse to skive off work for a week. By way of compensation for your sniffles, you could stretch it to a fortnight.

And the favourite way to comfort the symptoms is to go to bed with a hot-water bottle and a whisky.

Some chemists will try and persuade you to buy vitamin C tablets, zinc supplements or garlic pills for a cold. I know of no clinical evidence that they make any difference.

Millions of various kinds of headache pills are sold every day. They may mask the pain for a bit – you'll notice they're marketed as 'reliefs' not cures – but the real solution is to treat the cause. Most headaches have simple origins, like watching too much TV or having the wrong glasses.

You probably won't need indigestion pills and tablets either, if you watch your diet.

If you're in the habit of spending pounds and pounds at chemists' counters because you find that pills seem to work, remember the placebo effect. Most people start to feel better once they've taken a tablet even if there's no active ingredient in it.

This is why doctors dish out brightly coloured placebo pills, made of harmless starch and sugar, to patients who have conditions real drugs can't help.

Buy a book on old-fashioned herbal remedies. These are galloping back into favour. Scientific study shows some old wives may have had the right idea after all.

Got a runny nose? Paper tissues are bleached and impossible to recycle. Use a handkerchief. (It is, of course, quite easy to snaffle other people's tissues, as you pass their desk, at work, say.)

## It's Only a Cosmetic

Most eye make-up is tested on animals, usually by dosing the eyes of creatures that can't blink. Put it around that this is the reason you 'can't possibly' use eye-liner and mascara, and you'll save a useful lot of money. Younger teenagers who pester you to buy eye-shadow for them can be asked, 'Do you really want to stop a poor rabbit being able to see?'

Men also now have a wonderful green excuse for not buying wives and lady friends presents of exotic perfume. A few of the more famous brands are still made with musk oil. To get only a little of this, fifty musk deer have to be killed. Yet this is an endangered species. Cheaper perfumes use chemicals which simulate this oil.

You can also dissuade family members from buying perfume by idly asking, 'Does that favourite scent of yours have anything to do with that vivid purple rash I sometimes see on your neck?'

## Children

Disposable nappies are an environmental menace. It takes a big tree to produce only 1000 of them. And because of the chemicals added for absorbency, they take centuries to break down. Use conventional washable nappies and save cash.

You could also ask little Johnny if he thinks you ought to stop buying batteries for his gimmicky space-age toys. Tell him they use fifty times as much electricity to make as they actually provide. This means power stations release more greenhouse gas. And that, tell him, could soon mean that baby polar bears may have nowhere to live.

Many batteries contain cadmium and mercury, two noxious metals which are very hard to get rid of. If you buy your child a calculator, make sure it's solar-powered.

You can cut down on your spending on children, and keep their teeth in better condition, by teaching them that many jellies, cakes and biscuits have gelatine in them. As this is mainly gristle and bone, and all children love animals, it might just put them off. You might also drop it in that some red and pink sweets – including Smarties – are coloured with cochineal which is made from beetles.

It's easy to get out of taking children to zoos, circuses and dolphin aquariums. Tell them that lions and tigers don't like whips cracking over them, and that dolphins keep dying because they'd be far happier in the sea.

## Green Fingers

Stop buying bags of peat. A lot of it comes from Britain's wetlands – a fast-disappearing habitat for rare animals, birds and plants. Ordinary earth mixed with home-made compost is just as good for growing both outside and indoor plants.

If you haven't got room for a compost heap, leave household waste, grass cuttings, newspapers and leaves to rot in a black plastic sack. Abandon it in a sunny area. You'll be muck-spreading in just six weeks.

Allow nettles, dandelions and docks to grow in part of your plot. They draw butterflies, and other insects, which in turn attract birds. Nettles also entice finches. Supporting your local weeds also saves buying garden flowers. Put a sign up saying 'wildlife conservation area' to stop neighbours looking down their noses at your mini nature reserve.

## Greener Grass

You'll attract more butterflies and bees if you let your lawn grow a bit to allow clover and buttercups to appear. You now have less costs in running a mower and more Sunday afternoons free to count your money. And anybody seeing your slightly overgrown turf will praise your love of the environment.

Put out bowls of water to bring hedgehogs in. They munch slugs and insects, which saves you buying poisonous chemicals.

You won't feel as keen to buy cut flowers if you bear in mind that many blooms have been sprayed with insecticides. The chemicals could affect your health. Grow your own flowers for nothing.

## The Profit in Saving Paper

Ask neighbours to post their newspapers and magazines through your letter-box when they've read them. Say, 'We're trying to cut down on the demands we make on the rain forests.'

Request your children, in a kindly way, to give up their comics 'so that poor South American monkeys will still have somewhere to live.'

And you'll save even more wildlife (well, all right, postage) by paying all your bills by standing order.

Don't complain about getting junk mail. Very useful stuff, this. Use a paper knife to open envelopes carefully. Cut out neat labels from the bumph inside and send out your own letters. This little economy marks you out as a very caring citizen nowadays.

If your children try to persuade you to buy a parrot, or tropical fish, nip it in the bud by telling them that nine out of ten tropical birds die before they reach this country. And that five out of ten tropical fish expire within twelve months of being put in aquariums.

Should anyone try to railroad you into a French restaurant – often the most expensive place to eat – mention the fate of many an Indonesian frog which is called upon to give up its legs. What's left of the harmless creature often tries to crawl away to freedom.

And now to your biggest-ever green bonus. At one time, a car was seen as *the* prestige symbol. But it causes one half of the world's air pollution. So in these caring times you'll be more respected for not owning one. You can now scrounge lifts from friends and colleagues with a clear conscience.

How's that for a huge 'environmentally friendly' saving?

# How to Avoid Looking Mean

Men do not realise how great a revenue economy is.
(Non intelligunt homines quam magnum vectigal sit parsimonia.)
—*Cicero*

WHILE you are busy becoming rich by not being over-free with your money, you may, despite your best endeavours, be unfairly marked out for being mean. This would be catastrophic, because it would make it hard to get away with all your new-found skills learned in this book.

Luckily, suspicions can be allayed by a few artful dodges:

Bring a lot of home-grown vegetables and fruit into work and invite everyone to help themselves.

Accuse someone else in your circle of being mean, and conspicuously frown on the act. This will take suspicion away from you.

Use a carrier bag from a posh store, like Harrods, Moss Brothers or Cartier to carry stuff about in.

Smile and be charming when working a 'flanker' on somebody. (A flanker is a legal, but crafty way of gaining a pecuniary advantage.)

If you're with someone else, and you see a flag seller, rush across urgently and put something in the tin.

Ring up the 'speaking clock' and say in a voice which can be overheard in the office. 'Oh that's not much for all that trouble you took. You must send me an invoice for twice that amount.'

Stick higher price tags onto cheap presents before you wrap them. Attach them to inconspicuous places, as though you haven't noticed. Under a vase, say. Pencil in a bigger mark-up on any greetings card you send.

Secretly add your name to the card, if a friend or workmate receives flowers.

Take up a collection at work for a topical good cause: the latest earthquake victims, say. Even though you put in nothing yourself, you'll still be regarded as a paragon of generosity.

# Conclusion

Frugality embraces all the other virtues.
(Reliquas etiam virtutes frugalitas continet.)
—*Cicero*

THAT'S it. You're now privy to long experience of practical frugality – though I'd still like to hear of any more money-saving dodges you know about.

If you follow all the advice herein, you'll be well-clothed, well-fed, living in palatial surroundings, with a better job. Yet only a fraction of what you used to spend will ever leave your bank account.

All that extra money will make interest, and you should never look back. But don't pass this manual around, because the more people know these tips and tricks, the less effective they'll be. We can't all live like kings or queens.

And spare a thought for the author. All my friends, relatives and colleagues will probably stop talking to me, now they know exactly what I've been up to over the years.

Which is good, because I won't have to treat anyone with the money I make.

# Learning from Great Misers of the Past

Evading the stigma of being regarded as a cheapskate is vital if you're to escape the social disgrace of so many arch-frugalists in both fact and fiction. Because once it's generally known you are careful with money, you are dead: a social outcast.

Even the Bible gives a bad press to the more obvious penny-pincher (Revelation 3:17). So as a final fount of advice, it's worth listing some of the mistakes of the great misers, and where these blunders led them. We also examine other, equally famous people who managed to hide their frugality, and so remain highly respected to this day.

## Scrooge

Let's begin with the most celebrated tightwad of all – the happy inspiration for this guide. Yet Ebenezer can hardly be regarded as a success. His awful, spirited Christmas Eve would never have befallen him if he had splashed out occasionally. Or if he had refrained from spouting on about the hideous expense of Yuletide.

He was, as Dickens describes him, almost proud of his image, doing nothing to hide it from the world:

'. . . squeezing, wrenching, grasping, scraping, clutching and covetous. Hard and sharp as flint, from which no steel ever struck out generous fire.'

Scrooge also eventually let the side down by weakening. His downfall began when he bought a huge goose for somebody else. And then lashed out on humbugs and every other Christmas luxury from then on.

Scrooge's big failure as a frugalist is that he looked and behaved like one. The lesson we learn from him is to:

Wear expensive clothes (from charity shops).

Keep recommending the very best restaurants.

Always appear to be happy.

## Fagin

Here's another Dickens creation who lived up to one of the main planks in this book: a determination to live on others. This broken-down fence and leader of a gang of boy-thieves in Oliver Twist's London is not generally regarded as a miser. Though he adored money, he managed to avoid this label in the popular imagination, by being an extrovert who laughed a lot. You'd do well to ape him. Within reason, of course.

## King Midas

There's nobody better known for making a mess of being a frugalist than this legendary monarch of Phrygia. When the god Dionysus granted this Greek king a wish, he rashly asked that everything he touched should turn to gold. Then he almost starved to death because the only thing he could drink or eat after that was golden syrup. Or carrots spelt wrongly.

It's a wonder Midas managed to keep hold of any of his fabled wealth when you know how impetuous he was. He once told Apollo that he didn't think his music was as good as the minor deity Pan. For this, the top god gave Midas a set of donkey's ears.

The Midas touch warns all present-day money-lovers not to be hasty. Always take time to think your wheeler-dealing through. Is the return worth the effort? Are there unforeseen snags? Do you, like Midas, dislike gilt on your gingerbread?

## Vespasian

This is another well-known name to classical students of thrift. Vespasian, the first emperor of Rome after the Caesars, specialized in unusual taxes to raise cash. The most notorious of these was his unfair levy on public toilets. No doubt a lot of Super Scrooges would have to keep their legs crossed if this custom is ever revised.

## Henry VII

This king was *the* expert in making miserliness respectable. Historians fall over themselves to praise his skill at collecting wealth which, they argue, stabilized the country after the Wars of the Roses. Even Henry's portrait looks mean.

He began his avaricious reign by collecting the crown from a hawthorn bush after Richard III, who as a Yorkshireman should have known better, lost it on Bosworth Field.

Money was more important than land to Henry, very unusual among monarchs of the day. When in 1492 he wrested Brittany from Charles VIII of France, he settled for a big tribute instead.

When he died, he had taken so little out of the royal treasury that his heirs never looked back. 'Money is Power' was Henry's motto. An inspiration, if ever I heard one.

## Shylock

This unpopular citizen of Venice deserves respect as a freedom fighter for the Jewish faith. But because he kept banging on about having his pound of flesh, the poor chap is popularly perceived as money-mad.

Moral: if you want something, don't keep telling everyone that you do. Scheme quietly behind the scenes.

Shylock also came unstuck – and eventually lost half his fortune – because he let the profitless motive of revenge get in the way. You should never squander good money-making time getting your own back. If someone pulls a stroke on you, accept it with good grace, then adopt the technique to your own use.

## William Wordsworth

The Lakeland Poet is one of the most successful frugalists of all time, because very few people know he was at it. He set up the perfect smoke-screen for his meanness. He declared that it was only by spending little that he could identify with that poetic person – the rural peasant.

If you visit his very small home – Dove Cottage – you'll see his wooden bowl for visitor's calling-cards. (Contemporaries had posh porcelain versions.) His modest furniture was mainly second-hand, and he decorated upstairs with old newspapers.

Wordsworth, who was hugely popular in his day, demonstrates that if you can think of a plausible reason for not splashing out, no one will suspect your parsimony.

## Uncle Ebenezer of Shaws

Another famous writer who knew all about meanness, because he was Scottish, is Robert Louis Stevenson. His most famous miser is Ebenezer Balfour, a boo-and-hiss character in *Kidnapped*.

When his nephew calls to claim his father's inheritance, the disreputable old devil asks him to climb dark stairs to the guest room in his dreary home. The catch is that the room had fallen away from the house some time ago, and David nearly falls to his death. Afterwards the wicked uncle has more success by having the lad abducted.

It's apparent that Uncle Eb would never make a Super Scrooge. He lacks that vital quality: subtlety. Never go so far as to attempt to murder relatives or have them spirited away by sailors.

## Jack Benny

We can't end this book without mention of perhaps the only success-ful shatterer of the rule that superscrooging must be done discreetly. Comic genius Jack Benny made a fortune out of telling stories depict-ing him as a very, very, mean man.

He did it so often that very few people thought he was stingy at all. I bet he was, otherwise he would never have timed to perfection gags as good as this:

> Robber: 'Don't make a move. This is a stick up.'
> Benny: 'Mister, put down that gun.'
> Robber: 'Shut up. Now come on, your money or your life.'
> *(long pause)*
> 'Now look bud. I said your money or your life.'
> Benny: 'I'm thinking about it.'
> —The Jack Benny Show (NBC Radio, 1948)

Benny's apparent 'carefulness' also inspired other comics. Bob Hope said: 'They asked Jack Benny if he would do something for the orphanage. So he shot both his parents, and moved in.'

Jack's technique, it occurs to me, is going to be very useful if you are ever exposed irrevocably as the thrifty person you really are. Everyone will continue to love you if you make fun of yourself. And if you cheerfully admit you are a Super Scrooge, no one will really believe it anyway!